New Visions of Collective Achievement

New Visions of Collective Achievement

The Cross-Generational Schooling Experiences of African American Males

Foreword by Suzanne C. Carothers

Darrell Cleveland Hucks
Keene State College, New Hampshire, USA

SENSE PUBLISHERS
ROTTERDAM/BOSTON/TAIPEI

A C.I.P. record for this book is available from the Library of Congress.

ISBN: 978-94-6209-807-7 (paperback)
ISBN: 978-94-6209-808-4 (hardback)
ISBN: 978-94-6209-809-1 (e-book)

Published by: Sense Publishers,
P.O. Box 21858,
3001 AW Rotterdam,
The Netherlands
https://www.sensepublishers.com

Cover art and illustrations by Antonio Harry

Printed on acid-free paper

To Charetia Delores Hucks and Walter Cleveland Hucks, my parents, for their undying love on Earth and from Heaven.

TABLE OF CONTENTS

FOREWORD

What initiates the journey to a research problem ... the search, an inquiry into wanting to know more, a thirst to find an explanation about that which is often in plain sight but too often, overlooked because it is assumed to be "well that's just how it is?

I believe that authentic research questions come from an authentic place of caring, the trying to figure out "the why" of a situation, the inclusion of the voices of those in the situation, and, seeing the situation in its total context as a way to make meaning about a moment of behavior. Statistical data can offer insights into the *numbers* of what we see and a breakout of who displays the behavior. To thoughtfully respond to "the why" of many of the phenomena of human behavior we see, if we really want to understand "the why" of the behavior, *talking* with those who have the behavior is critical. Qualitative research becomes an important inquiry tool in seeking those answers. Or as John Szwed once wrote, "No amount of clinical study of alcoholics, for example, will establish how alcohol functions in the social setting in which it is consumed. In the same way, census data, no matter how accurate, will never tell us how a family functions –who is responsible for what, who teaches children what, and the like."[1] To learn these things requires interacting and talking with people about what matters to them.

With these thoughts in mind, I am remained of a bus ride that I once took which has implications for the origin/conception of research problems and the book you are about to read.

As I boarded the 104 Bus in New York City one spring afternoon going uptown on Broadway, I sat across from an adult and a child. Both were African American. Both were stylishly dressed. Both wore their hair in dreadlocks. Watching their interaction as we road together on this uptown bus, caused me to conclude that this was a mother and son. The boy appeared to be about eight or nine-years-old. Dressed in red jeans and an orange and black hoody on which there was writing and a dollar ($) symbol, this young boy smiled as he talked to his mother. She, in turn, was responsive to him – not only through the gestures in what she said, but the way in which she looked at him – the expressions on her face. Her eyes invited his words. After several blocks of stops as others entered and left the bus, the boy child lay his head on his mother's shoulder and quietly drifted off into sleep. His arm was linked into his mom's arm and his hoody covered his head as he slept peacefully. Slowly the bus made its way uptown. More stops along Broadway as we traveled. When the mom pressed the buzzer, she gently nudged her son saying, "Our stop is next." As his sleeping eyes opened, he awakened. Together, they left the bus.

Seeing this mother and boy child together set my mind in motion which led me to this book. As I looked at this innocent Black male child now, I wondered, in five, 10, or 15 years from now, what will be his trajectory? How will he see himself? How will others see him? This warm and tender moment of an innocent child that I have witnessed on this city bus is likely to be lost on a society that only knows Black boys as statistics, problems, and those to be feared. I questioned, when researchers set out to collect data on this child, what will constitute the data they collect? What will motivate their interest in him? What will they seek to know about his context? Will he have a voice in the story, the narrative that will be told about him? What is the story researchers will seek to tell about the trajectory of this Black male child?

The bus ride further encouraged me to think about journeys we take in life – where they start, what happens to them on the way, what becomes their destination? The book that follows is a story of a journey – a journey that began long before Hucks had taken a research methodology course in his doctoral program; long before he would become a teacher; before he would be a teacher educator; and, a professor in the academy. Much to the contrary, the research that informed this book is an outgrowth of a lived experience occurring during a childhood moment. It is a desire to understand that moment of behavior, to make meaning out of a witnessed contradiction observed in daily living. Children witness much in life that more often raises questions than offers honest explanations. Such was true in Hucks' case. As a child, he was an avid reader and good student in school. So when he once overheard his father struggle reading a passage from the Bible, at first he thought he was playing. As he listened longer, it became clear to him that his father was having difficulty reading. Even as a child, Hucks wondered how his father, whom he had experienced as a smart, capable man who taught him so many things, could have trouble reading? This unanswered question lingered with Hucks as he moved his life forward. No doubt, we are part of all of that which has come before us – a collective of experiences, places, events, and occurrences that shape, affect, and influence our direction.

New Visions of Collective Achievement: The Cross-Generational Schooling Experiences of African American Males is a book that has established a research problem which addresses an authentic question. It is the story of three generations of the schooling experiences of Black males. It is driven by an inquiry, a thirst to find an explanation about that which is in plain sight but often overlooked. It uses an initial *moment of contradiction* as a springboard, a starting place for additional questions and need to understand the broader context affecting the behaviors seen. It welcomes the voices of those whose lives are more often aggregated in statistical research findings, allowing them to speak ably for themselves. It is respectful of the stories that others tell about their lives. It bridges a gap between what some theories say about the behaviors of African American boys by offering new theoretical possibilities which have implications for practice. Thus, the book offers guidance for our work with African American boys in and beyond school.

As I revisit my bus ride on Broadway from the lens of *New Visions of Collective Achievement: The Cross-Generational Schooling Experiences of African American Males,* having observed the young Black male child who innocently slept on his mother's shoulder, I am hopeful that the lessons learned from the this book will protect, strengthen and guide this young child's trajectory into adulthood.

NOTE

[1] Szwed, John F. (1976). Anthropology now looks to the cities for field trips. *The New York Times,* February 22, IV 14:3.

Suzanne C. Carothers, Ph.D.
New York University

LIST OF TABLES

LIST OF FIGURES

ACKNOWLEDGEMENTS

This book is indeed a collective achievement. I offer my heartfelt thanks to the many people who have supported me during this process. I am deeply and most humbly grateful to Dr. Suzanne Carothers, my mentor. Suzanne, you willingly guided me through this journey and freely gave or your time, deep wisdom, and infectious humor. From the very start, you encouraged me to listen with my heart and allow my voice to come through this work. Your contributions are immeasurable. I thank Dr. Joseph McDonald for his support in helping me shape this work and his confidence in my abilities to tell this story. I thank Dr. Jacqueline Mattis for helping me see the strength of my research and collective achievement theory. I also thank James Oseland for recognizing the teacher in me many years ago, and I offer my appreciation to Drs. Margot Ely and Margaret Anzul for their contributions to my work. A sincere thank you to Dr. Emily Porschitz and family for your support and encouragement as I moved forward with this project. A special thank you to Matthew Ragan for your steadfast enthusiasm and loyal friendship.

I am indebted to Dr. Tracey Hucks for helping me imagine the possibilities of this research and for always being my hero. I am so grateful that we are family. I am also most grateful to Drs. Yolanda Sealey-Ruiz and Jody Polleck, my colleagues and dear friends; it has been my deepest honor to have both of you in my life. The two of you are simply amazing scholars and human beings. Your work inspires me to do my work better. To my uncle, Joseph Hucks, you have been more of a role model to me than you can ever imagine. Thank you for your wisdom and for being a constant reminder of the strength of the men in our family. I thank Charlene Richardson, my sister, and Zahir Watts, my nephew, for your love and support.

This work would not have been possible without the men and boys who trusted me with their stories: Jeremy, Shaun, Charles, James, Martin, Tyreek, Malik, Joshua, Tyrone, Jacob, and Larry. While these names are pseudonyms for each of you, I will never forget who you are. Your stories have changed my life for the better and will potentially change the lives of many others. To Benjamin Evidente, my dear friend, you have been like family from the very start. I don't know how I could have even imagined making this far without your unwavering support. You are a true friend. To Antonio Harry, the artist, thank you for capturing these images from the lives of the boys and men in this book. You have been eternally blessed with talent and true artistic vision. To Howard T. Reginald Miller, your love, kindness, and integrity have changed my life. And finally, I thank all of my family, friends, and former students and their families. You have helped me to uncover the pieces of this work; you are my educational legacy—you are with me each time I enter the classroom.

CHAPTER I

VISIONS OF AFRICAN AMERICAN MALES

When I was a young boy growing up in the South Bronx in the 1970s, the men in my family were like gods. They were deep thinkers, serious providers, and great protectors, and I watched them in awe. There was my Uncle Booker T., a smart and funny man who knew how to fix rusty cars with his strong hands. There was Uncle Elvin, a former military man who used to make sure that I never missed out on learning something new, be it how to play cards or how to pick out a good apple. And there was Granddaddy Jack, a hard-working man with a thick Southern accent, who always taught me that I could learn more by listening than by talking.

Most important of all was my father, Walter Cleveland Hucks, a robust, warm-hearted man who grew up poor in rural North Carolina in the 1940s. He moved to Harlem when he was eighteen and soon after met and married my mother, Charetia. I admired him enormously and we were always the best of friends. For me, the biggest treat with my father was riding around on summer days in the freight truck that he drove for a living. As he navigated his way through the busy streets of New York City, I was continually amazed at how he never once got lost.

Even with all that we did together and shared, I knew little about the details of my father's life as a child. What, for instance, was growing up like for him? What were his childhood dreams? When I sat next to him in that freight truck, I would tell him of my elementary school adventures and misadventures. He would laugh or look serious, depending on what I said. As I spoke, I was always hungry to know about what his experiences in school had been, but he never shared them with me. And when I would ask him outright, he was always somewhat evasive. He mentioned experiencing occasional problems with bullies, dealing with a few tough teachers, and having to walk long distances to and from school, but that was the extent of what he shared.

It wasn't until years later, when I was in high school that I learned my father couldn't read very well. I remember the day clearly. He was at home preparing to recite a passage from the Bible for an upcoming service in our church. I overheard him practicing in the next room. I listened as he slowly stumbled and faltered through the simplest of words. At first I thought he was joking, but I soon realized he wasn't. My father struggled to decode, much like a child learning to read. I didn't ask him about this at the time.

The enormity of the moment sent my mind into a tailspin. My father had proven to me countless times in the past how smart he was. He was a solid caregiver who knew how to save money. His intelligence was so clearly apparent to me. I remember how we would spend hours watching nature documentaries on TV. With ease, he would explain many of the concepts and ideas, which I myself always struggled with as a child. How was it possible that he couldn't read well? Had he not finished school? A few months later, my mother privately told me that while my father had indeed graduated from high school, he had continued to read at a grade-school level his entire life. I could only imagine the limitations this must have caused for him.

In the many years since then, I have tried to understand the relationship between my father's educational journey and my own. I was successful in school. I was a good student. I excelled at reading, social studies, and language arts. I went on to college and graduate school. My father obviously was not as successful educationally or academically. The same could be said for many of the African American males in my neighborhood. When I was growing up, I knew several young teenage boys who were turned off from education. I remember the boys with whom I played at the playground.

Historically, African American males bear the weight of timeless atrocities, experiencing a painful history of discrimination that continues to influence their marginalization in society. African American males are the least employed, the most imprisoned, and oftentimes, the most oppressed people in America (Davis, 2003; Majors & Billson, 1992; Noguera, 2003a; Ogbu, 1974). According to data from the United States Census Bureau (2010), 49.5% of African American males between grades 6 and 12 were suspended in 2007, while the National Center for Education Statistics (Aud, Fox, & KewelRamani, 2010) reported that in that same year, 12% of African American males ages 16 to 24 years old dropped out of high school. The U.S. Department of Justice (2009) has documented that over 40% of the American prison population consists of African American men. Statistics such as these clearly indicate a cause for better solutions to the challenges African American males face in schools and society.

In today's educational context of the "Achievement Gap" and "Disproportionality in Special Education," as well as the so-called "Crisis with Black Males" (Jackson & Moore, 2006; Pluviose, 2008; Watson, 2006), there is a longstanding debate about the engagement of and investment in African American boys in school (Noguera, 1996, 2003a; Mincy, 2006; National Urban League, 2008; Schott Foundation for Public Education, 2008; Watson, 2006). A significant body of research has supported quantitative measures, which reveal low-test scores, high dropout rates, and crime and incarceration statistics suggesting that African American males are not successful in school or in society (Duncan & Magnuson, 2005; Fryer & Levitt, 2006; Hoffman, Llagas, & Snyder, 2003; Schott Foundation, 2008; Toldson, 2008). In decades of school reform, from *Brown v. Board of Education* to the current era of the federal No Child Left Behind Act, and the recursive educational reforms these have ushered into our schools, African American males continue to occupy the bottom tiers in terms of achievement at all levels of school (Donnor & Schockley, 2010; Hughes & Bonner, 2006; Mincy, 2006; National Center for Education Statistics, 2007; Noguera, 2003a; Swanson, Cunningham, & Spencer, 2003). This concern raises the question of why, for generation after generation, African American males have not been successful academically.

In this book, I focus on the contextual factors that have influenced the cross-generational schooling experiences and achievement of African American males, revealing both the continuities and discontinuities that have been underexplored in past research, by using the voices of African American males to suggest directions for educational reform and future research.

SCHOOL

On many levels, the promise of educational advancement rendered in the 1954 landmark case *Brown v. Board of Education* has not been fully actualized. Years after *Brown*, education for some students did improve; for instance, some received far better access to resources and materials than their fathers ever received. For most, however, advancement never occurred. Despite recent reform efforts such as small schools, vouchers, charter schools, and the federal legislation of the No Child Left Behind Act (2001), a large number of African American males are still trailing behind other students in schools and in U.S. society. Today's standardized test achievement data demonstrate that African American males across all grade levels continue to lag significantly behind their counterparts. Legislators, administrators, and teachers still fail to offer constructive and engaging ways of addressing and countering these problems. In this way, African American boys are caught between a school system that holds low expectations and negative perceptions of their academic abilities and a society that often mirrors and distorts these images (Davis, 2003; Howard, 2008; Lewis & Moore, 2008; Noguera, 2003s; Osborne, 1999; Steele, 1990, 1998). This poses significant challenges for African American boys and their families. Many African American families continue to struggle for equal educational opportunities for their children. This is especially true for poor and working-class families living in inner cities and rural areas.

SOCIETY

The American public image of the African American family is one that is broken, weak, and unstable (Frazier, 1966; Hill, 2003; Lewis, 1966; Moynihan, 1965). Furthermore, the rise in the number of African American single-parent, female-headed households has had a tremendous impact on how African American fathers are viewed. These fathers are believed to be disengaged from their families or, worse, seen as deserters of their children. This negative public perception of absent African American fathers has raised much debate about the presence of positive male role models for African American boys (Hutchinson, 1997). In understanding and confronting these perceptions, people must examine the causes of this phenomenon, whether perceived or actual, so that we can begin to explore the structural changes in society and the impact they have had on our children. This exploration requires qualitative information that census data have not captured.

Qualitative research allows the lived experiences and perceptions of research participants to be captured in ways that quantitative research does not (Denzin & Lincoln, 2000; Glaser & Strauss, 1967; Lawler, 2002; Lincoln & Guba, 1985; Rubin & Rubin, 1995; Weiss, 1995). The increasing numbers of single-parent African American male- or female-headed households have only recently been studied (Hill, 2003). Findings from this study suggest that the changes in the structure of African American families belie the complexity of making generalizations about the influences that fathers have on their young children. The complexities of these relationships should be examined in ways that go beyond only knowing *how many* family members reside at the same address and start to address *why* this is occurring.

FAMILY

Family plays a significant role in the lives of children and a powerful influence on children's orientation to education and school. Many researchers have noted the crucial role the family has in shaping children's beliefs, perceptions, and values about their schooling (Kohn, 1999; Meier, 2002; Perry, Steele, & Hilliard, 2003; Sampson, 2002; Scanzoni, 1971; Thompson, 2003). Research suggests that parents' beliefs regarding past experiences of their own education are often passed on, directly or indirectly, to their children (Daniel & Effinger, 1996; Hale, 1994; Neblett, Chavous, Nguyên, & Sellers, 2009; Osborne, 1999; Sampson, 2002). Until recently, research focused on the intergenerational schooling experiences of African American males within the context of their families has been underexplored (Hucks, 2008). In 2009, Rowley and Bowman suggested that successful academic outcomes for African American males in higher education are impeded by "cross-generational family and student role strains"—specifically citing the absence of African American fathers and male role models as negatively influencing student motivation and peer risk behaviors, both in and out of school.

Furthermore, a limited number of studies have reported how African American role models actually do influence the children in their lives and their education (Hale, 1994; Hill, 2003; Perry, Steele, & Hilliard, 2003). Some of these studies have focused more on the relationships between African American mothers and their sons (Ferguson, 2001; Hale, 1982; Thompson, 2004), while others have focused on the role of fathers in their daughters' education (Draughn & Waggenstock, 1986). Still others have been intergenerational studies of the educational experiences of grandmothers, mothers, and daughters (Carothers, 1990; Daniel & Effinger, 1996; Sealey-Ruiz, 2007; Willie & Reddick, 2003). Only recently have studies begun to examine the impact of African American fathers on their sons' education (Harris, 1999; Polite & Davis, 1999; Scott, 1997).

While intergenerational studies about fathers, sons, and other male role models in the immediate and extended family may have offered males an opportunity to speak about education, these studies have not used a multi-theoretical framework as the current study does.

ACHIEVEMENT

Existing research shows that African American males are oftentimes most likely to be overrepresented in categories associated with school failure (Mincy, 2006; Moore, 2006; Noguera, 2008). The challenge for addressing this over-representation in underachievement is great and will require a level of engagement, investment, accountability, and achievement for all who play a role and have a stake in bringing about change for African American males.

The collective voices of African American males regarding their school and life experiences, and the issues and challenges they face, are missing from the literature. In examining the schooling experiences and achievement of African American males, educators and researchers have often not viewed them as being knowledgeable informants of their own experiences (Dance, 2002; Laubasher 2005; Mincy, 2006; Sampson, 2002; Sewell, 2000; Swanson, Cunningham, & Spencer, 2003; Thompson, 2004). Contrary to that approach, I asked African American boys and men to share their schooling experiences with me and they did.

My research documents the educational histories of a small number of urban African American boys, between the ages of 8 and 12, and those of the adult males in their immediate and extended families. I chose the age group of 8 to 12 for two reasons. First, it is a group that has not been intensively studied. Second, it is also the age group for whom standardized testing becomes the method of evaluating students' academic achievement in public schools—evaluations that resonate throughout the rest of these students' academic lives.

My study contributes to the research on African American males by closely examining the intergenerational educational experiences of boys and men in a select number of families. This research explored the connections that have gone unexamined by past researchers about the education and achievement of African American males. The goal of the study was to explore how African American males characterize their schooling experiences across generations, which is crucial for understanding the intergenerational conflicts, continuities, and interwoven experiences involved in their educational stories.

RESEARCH QUESTIONS

This study focused on understanding schooling experiences across generations from the perspectives of African American males. In exploring what their schooling experiences are across generations, this study investigated how their experiences shed light on the ways African American males were, and continue to be, served by the U.S. public educational system. In a quest to dig more deeply into these issues, I developed the following research questions:

- What are the educational stories of African American males?
- How do the educational experiences of previous generations of African American males inform those of the next generations?

- What "human capital" (parents, siblings, extended family, friends, and role models) do African American males use to navigate the public school systems?
- How do African American males evaluate their public school education?
- How do African American males see the value of their education and that of their families who send them to school?
- In what ways do African American males see the connections between their schooling experiences and life outcomes?

The yield from these research questions is the participants' multi-layered stories of their schooling experiences.

THE STORIES LIVES TELL

TELLING THE STORIES OF AFRICAN AMERICAN MALES

Framing the story of African American males and their families requires the inquiry of diverse literature. This literature review draws from historical, psychological, sociological, and anthropological research. Such a broad spectrum of research is necessary to identify major issues and factors when examining the intergenerational experiences of African American males. In addition to the social science literature, fiction and autobiographies were used in this dissertation because they introduce a unique perspective on the lives of African American males in the context of their schools and families. Authors such as James Baldwin, Amiri Baraka, and John Edgar Wideman weave their own life stories into fictional accounts, capturing the nuance of life for African American men living in the United States. The complexity of the lives of disenfranchised people has often been ignored in social science literature, reducing our understanding to simple equations; these fictional stories, on the other hand, counteract this simplicity and offer a rich context for understanding the human condition of people's lives.

Where They Stand: The View of African American Males Within Educational Settings

As stated previously, the obstacles African American males face are extreme, given that they are the least employed, the most imprisoned, and often the most oppressed (Davis, 2003; Majors & Billson, 1992; Noguera, 2003b). "Achievement" and "African American males" are terms usually linked together when low educational outcomes are discussed. Many researchers have noted that much of the data on African American males and their achievement are typically focused on low test scores, dropout rates, and crime and incarceration statistics (Dance, 2002; Hopkins, 1997; Noguera, 2003a; Osborne, 1999). The majority of existing quantitative achievement data is often used to support the notion that African American males are experiencing a serious crisis on multiple levels of society, especially in education. Of course, more than just statistics are involved in the daily lives and experiences of these boys and men, many of whom manage to succeed despite the challenges they face both in school and society.

When focusing specifically on young African American boys in schools, it is important to remember the cultural and social status of African Americans in the United States and the negative perceptions frequently associated with them. In her book *Tough Fronts*, L. Janelle Dance (2002) offered her view on the relationship between urban schools and African American boys and how educational institutions need to be more culturally responsive to their needs. She stated:

> Urban schools must acquire an empathetic understanding of what life is like for the students they serve. Otherwise, combating the negative aspects of street culture without an adequate and realistic understanding of how students relate to this culture and survive this culture is a losing battle: the casualties are reflected in high suspension, expulsion, and dropout rates for inner-city youth, especially Black and brown males. (p. 10)

Researchers suggest that African American males have countless personal stories to tell that speak of the obstacles they encounter in school—and in life (Anyon, 1997; Davis, 2003; Delpit, 1995; Majors & Billson, 1992; Noguera, 2003b; Polite & Davis, 1999; Sampson, 2002; Sewell, 2000; Smith & Wilhelm, 2002; Stevenson, 2004). In listening to and examining what African American male students have to say about their schooling and about those who teach them, schools will be able to offer sustainable ways to impact their educational experiences and outcomes positively.

Who They Are and Where They Live: The View of African American Males and Their Families

Since family is pivotal to a child's development, what then is the role of African American families in the development of their children? A large body of research has attempted to answer this question, documenting the significant role that the family plays in students' achievement and orientation to education and school (Davis, 2003; Hale, 1982; Hill, 2003; Kunjufu, 1995; Lawrence-Lightfoot, 2003; Ogbu, 1974; Sampson, 2002; Thompson, 2003). From their inception as slaves in America, much has been written about the African American family. Research has been conducted about African American families from the 1800s to the 1900s, including a seminal study written in the 1940s by E. Franklin Frazier (1966), which offers a challenging perspective on African Americans that had not existed before. This study identified the strengths of the African American family that had gone unrecognized until then. This investigation proliferated even more in the 1960s with the publication of the *Moynihan Report* by Daniel P. Moynihan (1965). Moynihan explored African American families and attributed their problems to the "inherent feebleness" of their family. Unfortunately, this negative perspective superseded Frazier's work and has led many in the popular media and the government to place blame on the African American family for the problems they face.

In a recent article, Leswin Laubasher (2005) counteracted these perspectives, arguing that the research on African American men is largely centered on crisis and pathology. He suggested that this crisis is manufactured and is a result of the negative research on the deficits of African American men, thus sustaining a societal misrepresentation rather than truly understanding the realities of interlocking families and how they are affected by institutionalized racism. The literature itself on these crises played a significant role in perpetuating an oppressive representation of African American males in society. Laubasher thus called for the development of research that does not support the problematic societal views of African American males and instead focuses on their strengths.

Other literature also explored the impact of relationships within African American families. A socio-psychological study conducted by Diane Hughes and Deborah Johnson (2001) focused on the racial socialization experiences of 94 parent-child dyads. The authors explored the transactional processes between parents and children, focusing on the child's identity exploration and their parents' racial socialization. In doing so, the authors studied the effects of the unfair treatment of the children in school. They also found that the children's views of discrimination and their ways of questioning this oppression had an effect on how their parents talked to them about race. This was significant in that it showed racial socialization as being transactional. One limitation of the study, however, was that the sample was taken only from affluent African American parents. It would be interesting to see if these same transactional results appear with families from varied socio-economic backgrounds.

While research on African American families has increased, much of the research has historically focused on the influence of mothers and grandmothers—and not fathers and grandfathers—on their children's education. The research on familial influences and school experiences from the males' perspectives, specifically the school experiences of fathers and sons, is seriously lacking in scope. Some studies have explored the schooling experiences of African American males at the secondary or college level, but more connections need to be made to previous elementary school experiences and how these experiences relate to the older males in their families.

The intergenerational school experiences of African American males have also not been looked at closely in the existing research on African American males. These holes in the literature may be tied to the societal view of the "absent father" or the so-called "lack of male role models" believed to plague the African American community. To counteract this, several studies have explored this negative misconception of African American fathers. One study by Roberta L. Coles (2002) examined the parenting methods of a small group of single African American fathers and their experiences as the primary caregivers of their children. Coles found that the men's past experiences throughout their life had a significant impact on their roles as fathers in raising their children in that these experiences informed their beliefs and perceptions about their children's current experiences both inside and outside of school. The findings of this study also suggested that the fathers' social networks had a significant impact on the parenting choices they made. Pedro Noguera (2003a) also explored this phenomenon in *City Schools and the American Dream*, in which he addressed the inadequate resources African American males have for social capital, which is the social network people need to access things they require. This dearth of social capital thus has tremendous negative influences on the experiences of poor children and their families in and out of school.

In terms of the intergenerational literature on African American males, the research has, for the most part, been centered on the influences of ethnic identity on educational, psychological, and cultural struggles. I have been unable to find studies that specifically examine the impact of intergenerational, familial relationships. While a growing body of literature is looking at the issues and challenges encountered by African American fathers (Clayton et al., 2003; Hamer, 2001; Mincy, 2006), nothing yet addresses education in a systematic, qualitative way, because this research primarily centers on the challenges fathers face as economic providers.

Some work has been conducted to explore the issues of masculinity and gender role development in African American men (Sewell, 2000; Wade, 1996), but few studies have focused on how these issues impact school experiences within the context of the family. In *African American Teens Discuss Their Schooling Experiences*, Gail Thompson (2002) explored the school experiences reported by teenage African American male and female students. Although the students interviewed in this study were in high school, many of them reported significant experiences that happened during their elementary school years that they felt negatively impacted their later experiences in school. According to Thompson, "Tracking, starting in elementary school, not only contributes to low achievement among African American students but it also appears to have a strong effect on subsequent schooling experiences" (p. 164).

Due to the cultural and educational history of African American males, and the achievement issues they continue to face in school, there is a pressing need for research that explores how different generations of African American males have experienced school, how they relate these experiences across generations, and how this impacts their achievement. According to Bowman and Gadsen (1999), "Part of the solution to the problems facing young, poor African American males is located in schools. However, educational-reform discussions seldom address the special risks faced by African American males and are marked often by conflicting assumptions" (p. 178). These conflicting assumptions include misperceptions that African American children come from broken homes with families that do not value education, which ultimately causes behavioral problems and academic deficiencies.

Adding to Bowman and Gadsen's research are several studies that have focused on the impact of community and family on children's schooling experiences. Jeremy Price's (1999) ethnographic-sociological study detailed the school experiences of two young African American men. Price explored the varying effects that teachers, graduation, and peer relationships had on the participants' masculine and racial identities. The interviews revealed how gender, class, and race were woven throughout all levels of these students' personal and social experiences. The study demonstrated these two men, who came from the same community, assigned very different meanings to their experiences both inside and outside of school. Their personal histories, their peer groups, and the context of the social institutions they entered shaped the meanings they developed. In this way, Price urged the need for a theoretical framework that moves beyond the historical one-dimensional images of African American men. This study is significant in that it revealed how the complexities of race, gender, and class impact African American meaning-making systems.

Another sociological study by Dena Philips Swanson, Michael Cunningham, and Margaret Beale Spencer (2003) explored the effect of affective-and cognitive-linked developmental transitions on academic achievement and outcomes for African American males. Consisting of 219 ninth and tenth graders, data for this study were gathered using three different questionnaires that measured participants' experiences and their negative and positive inferences. The authors explored the various stereotypes of African American males in society and the impact of family, school, and community on their affective and cognitive development. The authors suggested that to assist these males in positive and constructive ways, educators need to seek out and gain a thorough understanding of the significance of these factors on their lives.

These authors also used a human development perspective to examine the academic achievement patterns and outcomes that the participants in the study experienced. They found that hyper-masculine behaviors such as bullying and fighting were often exhibited by students in response to negative schooling experiences. As such, they advocated for interventions that not only attempt to change behaviors, but require a change in the environments that produce these responses. This research is crucial because of its developmental perspective and how this applies to African American male achievement and the complexities involved in addressing the issues faced by students and the schools that serve them.

Class also significantly impacts the life and school experiences of African American males. Based on ethnographic data of 8- to 10-year-old White and Black children, a study by Annette Lareau (2002) explored the effects of social class on family childrearing practices. Using data collected from interviews and observations of children and their parents, the findings from this study indicated that middle-class parents were more involved in activities that developed their children's reasoning skills and provided more organized leisure activities. On the other hand, working-class and poor parents provided an environment that facilitated children's natural growth, but they allowed their children to make more decisions about leisure activities. Lareau also found that Black middle-class families had more resources and strategies available for dealing with issues of racial discrimination than their working-class and poor counterparts. Another difference was that children from middle-class families developed a greater sense of entitlement when dealing with institutional settings, while working-class and poor families did not share this feeling. This research demonstrated the impact that class and family dynamics have on children's potential life outcomes.

Lareau conducted another sociological study with Erin McNamara Horvat (1999) that centered on the intersection of race and class, looking at third grade African American children and their parents. Conducting case studies based on classroom observations and interviews, the research suggested that White parents of students in schools that are predominantly White had less concern when dealing with institutional problems than African American parents who may be coming from historically-based patterns of racial discrimination. The researchers found that race has power regardless of social class in schools, and they pointed to the significance of class and race on social reproduction and the ways in which individuals activate cultural capital. Finally, the authors also suggested that the past experiences of parents and their children influenced their responses to racial discrimination.

AFRICAN AMERICAN BOYS AND THEIR SCHOOL EXPERIENCES

For African American male students at every grade level, the discontinuity between home and school has a tremendous impact on their schooling experiences and academic achievement (Delpit, 1995; hooks, 2004; Kotlowitz, 1991; Noguera, 2003b; Rist, 1973). It is important to understand the variety of factors that shape and influence this discontinuity as well as any continuity, and the ways in which we serve African American males in the public school system.

Before looking at the school experiences of African American boys, it is crucial to explore racial identity and the socialization of African Americans. The first study, conducted by Ron Eyerman (2004), addressed racial identity and presented a structure for a theory of cultural trauma, focusing on how the history of slavery in the Americas has impacted the development of African American identity. Eyerman explained that after the Civil War, Black intellectuals created the term "African American" in response to the unfulfilled promise of full integration and further rejection (individual and collective) by American society. The author looked at the concepts of collective memory and collective identity, and used historical references to shed light on the impact of cultural trauma on both the individual and the collective African American culture. By looking at historical narrative frameworks and their representation, we can gain a stronger understanding of the impact of generational memory and how it is passed on.

Psychologists Richard Allen and Richard Bagozzi (2001) also conducted a study that investigated the framework of African American belief systems across three different age groups. They posed several key hypotheses informed by the historically negative treatment of African Americans by those belonging to the dominant culture. On a fundamental level, the researchers found that African American belief systems were informed by their sense of self and their worldview. The model they used to explore this issue focused on African American belief systems on both the individual and group levels. Using a multistage sampling method for this psychological study, the findings indicated that there was a significant difference in the degree of group identity between age cohorts based on whether they were born pre- or post-Civil Rights era. It was also found that individual and group African American identity was related to the views and values of the larger society across age groups. This understanding of individual and group identity and belief systems is crucial for our understanding of the school experiences of African American males.

One of the few related studies that focused specifically on young African American boys was conducted by Ann Annette Ferguson (2001). Following a group of 11- and 12-year-old African American boys in an urban setting, Ferguson brought to light a pressing need to look at the early formative school years of African American males. She discussed how her young participants were already labeled as academically challenged by their teachers, leading to many negative schooling outcomes. Furthermore, she revealed the continuum of fathers in her study from present and wielding influence, to absent and how this impacted the children and their academic achievement.

Ferguson's work is indicative of the major challenges that African American boys face in terms of their educational achievement. Stereotyping by those in positions of authority, including teachers, administrators, and security officers, is often due to the media's labeling of African American males as aggressive and violent (Hill, 2003). These media influences have a profound impact on how the behavior of African American males is viewed by those outside of their ethnic group. According to Feagin and Vera:

> Symbolic violence resides in relentless stereotyping, the media's exclusionary standards of beauty, and the educational system's insensitivities to the needs of multicultural communities. Symbolic violence can include White [police] officers' hostile words and body language, which reveal disrespect for Black people and culture, as well as White officers' show of force in Black communities when they stop and interrogate Black men just because they are Black. Symbolic violence is expressed in images of Blacks as inferior or as "gorillas in the mist." Many Whites in all sectors of society acquiesce or participate in acts of symbolic violence even though they disapprove of physical violence. (in Dance, 2002, p. 139)

This insensitivity on behalf of teachers and administrators towards children of color has a profound impact on student experiences, classroom environment, and the overall school climate (Rist, 1970).

In terms of achievement, according to a sociological study by Vernon C. Polite (1999), African American males who attended the suburban high school that he studied felt that most of their counselors and teachers had not made an effort to challenge them academically, particularly their math teachers. These participants also felt that a "caring school environment" had not been created by their counselors or teachers. Furthermore, Polite suggested that these participants' experiences reflected the high school experiences of African American students throughout the nation.

Pedro Noguera (2003b) also explored how environmental and cultural factors influenced African American boys' behavior and performance in school. He looked at the role personal perception and group identity play on academic achievement. Noguera offered constructive ways to address the problems these boys faced in school and in society. Moreover, he raised the issue of generational, racial, and class differences as a source of difficulty for communication between adults and children. Because of these disparities, Noguera advocated for additional resources and support systems both inside and outside of schools to create conditions that produce academic success, thus meeting the needs and growth of African American boys on multiple levels.

Another article by Jason W. Osborne (1999) also offered possible courses of action that may be used to promote boys' identification with academics and improve their educational achievement. The author examined three prominent theories (Steele's stereotype threat model, Ogbu's cultural-ecological perspective, and Majors and Billson's "cool pose" theory) that addressed factors impacting achievement. These three theories took into account the social and cultural landscapes that African American males must navigate in school and in their communities—landscapes that affect the ways they may relate to academics. This has tremendous implications for schools and teachers when considering how they plan for and implement curriculum, interventions, and assessments.

WHERE AFRICAN AMERICAN MALE STORIES ARE TOLD: (AUTO) BIOGRAPHICAL AND FICTIONAL LITERATURE

Fictional and autobiographical literature provides examples of the influence of family on children's school experiences and their understandings of education. Here is where we find the intergenerational stories of African American men. Historically, as stated previously, social science literature has ignored the lives of disenfranchised people; to counteract this, many African American writers have written both autobiographical and fictional accounts to unravel and expose their experiences. Richard Wright (1945), W.E.B. Du Bois (1973), James Baldwin (1985), Toni Morrison (1977), Ralph Ellison (1995), Alice Walker (2003), and many others have told stories of struggle and resilience of African Americans from slavery to the present day.

One African American author in particular, Alex Haley (1976), in his compelling book *Roots*, offered one of the most powerful views of African American life across seven generations of his family. This account started with the capture of his ancestor by slave traders in Africa who brought him to America. What stands out most poignantly is the powerful familial relationships that sustain, despite the horrendous conditions of slavery. Furthermore, Haley highlighted how children's learning and development occurred within the context of family and community, despite what slave owners sought to extinguish.

African American writers continue to tell the stories of what life is like for African American males at various ages and walks of life, providing varied lenses to understand African American experiences in post-slavery U.S. society. James Mc Bride (1996) in *The Color of Water* offered a detailed account of his life growing up in the Red Hook projects of Brooklyn and the influence of his bi-racial family, his peers, and the environment on his life at home and in school. Similarly, in *Raising*

Fences, Michael Datcher (2001) shared his life experiences growing up on and off the streets of Los Angeles.

In Geoffrey Canada's (1998) *Reaching Up for Manhood*, Bill Cosby's (1986) *Fatherhood*, and John Edgar Wideman's (1994) *Fatheralong*, African American men also told stories about the intergenerational relationships they had with their sons and the importance of developing and maintaining positive and constructive connections that helped their children overcome obstacles in school and in society. The following statement at the close of Wideman's book encapsulates the sentiments shared by many African American men: "The powers and principalities that originally restricted our access to the life free people naturally enjoy still rise like a shadow, a wall between my grandfathers and myself, my father and me, between the two of us, father and son, son and father. So we must speak these stories to one another" (p. 197).

This type of literature counters greatly to most of the social science literature that has historically focused on only single, one-dimensional aspects of the lives of African American males, dangerously hypothesizing wide-scale implications about their performance, achievement, and life trajectories. Contrastingly, fictional and autobiographical literature sheds light on the complexity of issues defining the circumstances in which African American males find themselves. Inspired by this literature, my research also lifts up and celebrates the voices of African American males, specifically unraveling the complexities of their educational experiences.

IN SEARCH OF A THEORETICAL GROUNDING

As an African American male researcher, I found that multiple theories and concepts resonated with my own schooling experiences and the experiences of other African American males in my family and community. I quickly recognized that not one theory, concept, or perspective could, or should, be applied to the complexity of African American males. The idea of framing these multiple theories collectively, not separately, made more sense and told a richer story.

One theoretical framework of this study comes from Jason Osborne's (1997) perspective on disidentification with academics. He suggested that the educational achievement of African American males is directly related to whether or not they identify with their education. According to Osborne (1999), the self-esteem of "identified students" is more strongly correlated with academic outcomes than it is with "disidentified students" (p. 557). In other words, students who feel connected to what they are learning in school will perform better academically as a result of this connection.

Other related theories and perspectives have contributed to this study's framework. Drawing from psychological research, Claude Steele's (1992, 1997) stereotype-threat model suggested that if one belongs to a minority group in which there are negative stereotypes about that group's academic ability, then that group's academic performance in school is adversely affected.

I also used John Ogbu's (1997) cultural-ecological perspective, which hypothesized that the home culture and community with which a student identifies impacts his school performance. Ogbu also suggested that students coming from a culture that has viewed them as being oppressed may also view school as a continuation of that oppression. Ogbu moreover hypothesized that often the belief and value systems of African American males and their families are in conflict with those of educators and administrators at their schools. In *The Next Generation,* Ogbu (1974) discussed this conflict of opposing belief systems, claiming:

> The White belief system, which contributes the other half of the self-fulfilling prophecy in education of subordinate minorities, consists of both folk and "scientific" definitions of the subordinate minorities as intellectually and culturally inferior to Whites. Whites confirm their folk beliefs and "scientific" theories by pointing to the high proportion of school failures and low scores on intelligence tests (IQ) among subordinate minorities. These beliefs and theories form the basis on which the schools sort and classify children from subordinate minorities, a classification that often marks the children as failures before the school actually teaches them anything. It is important to remember that teachers participate in the belief system of the dominant Whites rather than that of the subordinate minorities, and that their definition, classification, and treatment of children are determined by that belief system. (p. 14)

Ogbu demonstrated the serious need to examine belief systems at work on both sides of the home-school equation. Furthermore, the need for open, constructive, and continuous communication among students, teachers, parents, and administrators is the only way that possible solutions for the problems faced by all students, especially young African American males, will ever be identified and put into practice to improve their school experiences and lives (Delpit, 1995; Ladson-Billings, 1994; Lawrence-Lightfoot, 2003; McDonald, 1996).

Adding to the work of Ogbu, Steele, and Osborne is the "cool-pose" theory envisioned by Richard Majors and Janet Billson (1992). This theory suggested that African American males adopt a pose of acting "cool" in school as a coping mechanism for the challenges they face. Lastly, I used Pedro Noguera's (2003a) environmental and cultural perspective, which explored the interaction of harmful environmental and cultural factors that have an impact on young African American males both in and outside of school. Throughout my study, I examine how these theories and perspectives play out in the intergenerational narratives of African American males within the context of their families, highlighting how the components of this collective theoretical framework are revealed in the stories of their school experiences.

Based on these theories, it becomes clear that the problems faced by African American males within schools are complex. Many factors lead to discontinuity that impacts the educational and life outcomes of this population. I have attempted to identify some of the major factors through this study. In combination, they are difficult to address without a deeper knowledge of how these factors work together to impact achievement. With this in mind, researchers need to investigate the complex strength and influence of these factors across different stages of children's development and across the life span. Furthermore, researchers need to understand how these factors shift and hold across generations. According to Ruth Benedict (1934),

> The life history of the individual is first and foremost an accommodation to the patterns and standards traditionally handed down in his community. From the moment of his birth the customs into which he is born shape his experience and behavior. By the time he can talk, he is the little creature of his culture, and by the time he is grown and able to take part in its activities, its habits are his habits, its beliefs his beliefs, its impossibilities his impossibilities. (p. 3)

Benedict demonstrated the importance of understanding how customs and beliefs are established, arguing that cultural institutions play a significant role in supporting or impeding individual progress. Thus, these institutions more effectively serve dominant groups and subordinate minority groups from having their needs met because of the negative beliefs held by those in power.

As Margaret Mead concluded in Alan Dundes' (1968) *Every Man His Way*: "If we are to build a world in which a variety of cultures are orchestrated together so as to produce a viable social order, we need intensive exploration of the types of clarification and types of presentation which will increase understanding between pairs of cultural groups and then among more complicated groupings" (p. 534). Franz Boas (1982) emphasized that "a synthesis of the elements of culture must be undertaken that will give us a deeper insight into its nature" (p. 265). I focused on family elements as reported by the males themselves.

Based on these theoretical frameworks, it becomes clear that psychological, sociological, environmental, and cultural factors are closely related and interwoven. This requires a thorough understanding of African American families and the schools their boys attend (Cross, 1991). If African American boys are to be successful in school and society, we need a more thorough knowledge of how education is viewed and practiced by the older males in their families and communities who hold key positions to the boys' conceptions of schooling and achievement.

THEORETICAL FRAMEWORK

The current study contributes to the research on African American males by closely examining the intergenerational educational experiences of boys and men in a select number of families. This research explored the connections that have gone unexamined by past researchers between education and achievement of African American males. The goal of the study was to explore how African American males characterize their schooling experiences across generations, which is crucial for understanding the intergenerational conflicts, continuities, and interwoven experiences involved in their educational stories and how they impact students' academic performance in schools today.

Due to my shared ethnicity with the participants in the study, years of elementary school teaching of African American boys, and engaging with the literature on African American males, I quickly realized that not one isolated theory, model, or perspective could, or should, be applied to the complex lives of African American males. This design was based upon preliminary conversations with African American males prior to the current study, when I discovered that one theory or concept on its own could not capture the range of factors that inform the schooling experiences of African American males on an intergenerational scale. But enacting them as a collective did allow for a more open-ended research design that captured the intergenerational continuities and discontinuities that exist among the participants, and also gave rise to this new theory of collective achievement. The idea of seeing the African American boys collectively, not separately, made more sense and told a richer story. The following researchers provided this collective framework:

- Osborne's (1997, 1999) perspective on disidentification with academics suggested that the educational achievement of African American males is directly related to whether or not they identify with academics.
- Steele's (1992, 1997) stereotype-threat model suggested that if one belongs to a minority group in which there are negative stereotypes about that group's academic ability, then that group's academic performance in school will be adversely affected.
- Majors and Billson's (1992) "cool pose" theory suggested that African American males adopt a pose of acting "cool" in school as a coping mechanism for the challenges they face.
- Noguera's (2003a) environmental and cultural perspective suggested that the interaction of harmful environmental and cultural factors have an impact on young African American boys both in and out of school.
- Ogbu's (1997) cultural-ecological model suggested that the home culture and community with which a student identifies will impact his school performance. He also argued that students, coming from a culture that has viewed itself as being oppressed, may view school as a continuation of that oppression.

The current study intended to address the deficit of African American male voices in the literature by engaging with African American males from within the same family unit across generations through qualitative interviews and observations in their homes and communities. This study focused on understanding schooling experiences across generations from the perspectives of African American males. In exploring what their schooling experiences are across generations, this study investigated how their experiences shed light on the ways African American males were and continue to be served by the U.S. public educational system. In a quest to delve more deeply, I used the following questions as a guide to framing the study and generate interview questions:

- What are the educational stories of African American males?
- How do the educational experiences of previous generations of African American males inform those of the next generations?
- What "human capital" (parents, siblings, extended family, friends, and role models) do African American males use to navigate the public school systems?
- How do African American males evaluate their public school education?
- How do African American males see the value of their education and that of their families who send them to school?
- In what ways do African American males see the connections between their schooling experiences and life outcomes?

METHODOLOGY

The current study documented over a two-year period (spanning six to eight months per family), through a series (two to four per individual) of in-person interviews conducted in participants' home environments, the educational histories of a group of urban African American boys, between the ages of eight and twelve, and those of the older males in their immediate and extended families. The age group of eight to twelve was specifically chosen for two reasons: First, it is a group that has not been intensively studied around issues of schooling. Second, it is also the age group for which standardized testing becomes the method for evaluating students' academic achievement in public schools—evaluations that resonate throughout the rest of these students' academic lives.

INTRODUCTION TO METHODOLOGICAL THEORIES

My research study was anchored in the methodological approach of Grounded Theory (Strauss, 1970). Founded by Anselm Strauss (1970), this theory is the foundation for qualitative inquiry. Bogdan and Biklen (2003) believed that "qualitative researchers set up strategies and procedures to enable them to consider experiences from the informants' perspectives" (p. 7).

While employing qualitative research, this study was also grounded in ethnographic methods. As discussed by Irving Seidman (1998), qualitative research and ethnographic approaches allow researchers to understand the complex lives of their participants. Seidman (1998) suggested, "Although anthropologists have long been interested in people's stories as a way of understanding their culture, such an approach to research in education has not been widely accepted" (p. 7).

An essential quality of qualitative and ethnographic methods is using in-depth interviews, which were a critical part of my dissertation in understanding the schooling experiences of African American males. Seidman (1998) made a particularly strong argument in support of conducting qualitative interviews:

> Because in-depth interviewing uses a method that is essentially open-ended, preparation, planning, and structure are crucial. Each interview requires a series of instantaneous decisions about what direction to take. Researchers entering an interviewing situation without a plan, sense of purpose, or structure within which to carry out that purpose have little on which to base those decisions. Without a thoughtful structure for their work, they increase the chance of

distorting what they learn from their participants and of imposing their own sense of the world on their participants rather than eliciting theirs. (p. 33)

While I attempted to keep the interviews as open-ended as possible, I did have a set of questions for eliciting essential narratives from my participants. At the same time, I tried to give my participants as much as freedom as possible in articulating their experiences. Bogdan and Biklen (2003) explained the importance of this kind of interviewing process:

> The open-ended nature of the approach allows the subjects to answer from their own frame of reference rather than from one structured by prearranged questions. In this type of interviewing, questionnaires are not used; while loosely structured interview guides may sometimes be employed, most often the researcher works at getting the subjects to freely express their thoughts around particular topics. (p. 3)

The interview structures explained by Bogdan and Biklen as well as Seidman suggest that one goal of qualitative interviewing research is to reveal the complexities of the human experience. Therefore, careful selection of methods must be thoroughly considered before engaging in the process.

PARTICIPANT SELECTION

I used several criteria for selecting participants for my study. First, all boys were African American and attended public elementary schools in a large urban community. The ages of the boys ranged from eight to twelve and all were descendants of African slaves in the United States, as opposed to children of first-generation African or Caribbean immigrants. Another criterion was that at least three generations of males were available to be interviewed in each family. Furthermore, all participants signed informed consent letters, which included their agreement to participate within the study. The boys and their family members received age-appropriate letters explaining the purpose of my research study. Participants were informed that participation in the study was strictly voluntary and they could withdraw from the study at anytime. Pseudonyms were also given to each participant to ensure confidentiality and protect his privacy.

The Quest for Families

From the beginning of writing my research proposal, the questions of how, when, and where I would find African American families who were willing to participate in my study was a major concern. When I asked for assistance from colleagues and friends, I received a variety of responses. Some seemed to think it would be so easy for me to find African American males eager for the opportunity to take part in my research. Others seemed a bit more skeptical and offered solutions to the challenges of finding African American men. Fortunately, others went as far as making phone calls to their friends, families, and neighbors on my behalf.

I traveled through Black neighborhoods with several copies of my recruitment flyers, which provided a brief yet thorough description of my study as well as contact information for interested participants. I also visited barbershops for fathers and beauty salons for mothers, hoping that these women would be strong advocates for encouraging the men to participate. When these two strategies still did not produce the hoped-for results, I began to visit local museums, libraries, community centers, and churches. In short, I turned many stones seeking potential participants, yet not all my efforts were successful.

Another strategy for recruitment was meeting face to face with a very influential and well-known church leader at a historic Black church. After explaining my research to a female, junior pastor through several email exchanges, she finally told me to call the head pastor's secretary to make an appointment. On the day of this appointment, armed with a slew of flyers, I arrived half an hour early for our meeting. The junior pastor ushered me into his immense office with wall-to-wall carpeting and polished dark wood furniture. Taking a seat opposite his desk, I waited patiently for the head pastor to finish his phone call. He shook my hand and asked me to explain my research study. His face seemed stern as he sat listening to my story and the nuances of my research. Once I was done, a smile crept over his face and he said that he would take my flyers and distribute them to the congregation in the next Sunday church program. I thanked him for his time and quickly gathered up my belongings.

On my trek back to my apartment, I felt confident that I would probably have more participants than I needed as a result of this meeting. But once again, time revealed that I was off the mark: I never heard from anyone at this church. A parishioner friend of mine even told me that she had never seen any of my flyers in the church. I was puzzled and disappointed, but did not let these dead ends stop my quest for participants.

I then reached out again to the friends, who put the word out to people they knew would fit my criteria for participation. Hoping that word-of-mouth and personal connections would yield better results, I spent the next couple of months following up on any leads. Finally, success prevailed, leading me to three families who all agreed to participate in my study: the Andersons, the Wallaces, and the Freemans.

DATA COLLECTION AND ANALYSIS

A major goal of this research was to document the rich, vivid portraits of the schooling experiences of African American males from interview data and then analyze these narratives for trends and significant findings. Given the nature of qualitative research, data collection and analysis were recursive activities; one interview often informed the approach and questions I would include in subsequent interviews.

Interviews and Participant Observations

As stated previously, interviews were a crucial aspect of my research. Bogdan and Biklen (2003) believed that by asking questions, we can "discover 'what they [participants] are experiencing', 'how they interpret their experiences', and how they themselves structure the social world in which they 'live'" (p. 7). This is, indeed, a primary goal of qualitative researchers. Furthermore, I used methods of active interviewing as proposed by Holstein and Gubrium (1995) who explained that this kind of conversation allows both interviewer and informant to use the "dynamic interplay between the two, to reveal both the substance and process of meaning-making in relation to research objectives" (p. 76).

Using these methods, over a six-month period I conducted interviews with three families, spending spent nearly two months with each family before moving on to the next. Once I obtained permission from the participants, I tape recorded and transcribed all the interviews. In conducting these interviews, I attempted to make the process as collaborative as possible. As Ely et al. (1991) explained, "The major purpose of an in-depth ethnographic interview is to learn to see the world from the eyes of the person being interviewed. In striving to come closer to understanding people's meanings, the ethnographic interviewer learns from them as informants and seeks to discover how they organize their behavior" (p. 58). Although the participants generally directed the interview, this did not imply that I was merely a passive receiver of the participants' stories nor that I used highly structured questions. On the contrary, I fully engaged in the conversations while simultaneously using open-ended questions to "unearth valuable information that tight questions do not allow" (p. 66). To be effective in conducting these kinds of interviews with informants, researchers must also draw upon their own prior knowledge in formulating these open-ended questions. More importantly, I attempted to create and revise questions that were consonant with or arose from the ongoing data I collected throughout the study (Ely et al, 1991).

While the data from the interviews were used to answer the study's primary research questions, I also used the interviews to expand my understanding of African American males and their school experiences more holistically. Tunnell (1998) explained:

Ethnographic interviewing encompasses more than simply learning about a particular problem or population. It is an ongoing lesson about how to relate to divergent groups of people, how to establish rapport, how to win confidence, and how to assist them in opening up and revealing those subtle complexities of social life that can only be tapped through qualitative methodologies. (p. 136)

In this way, the other goal of my study was to establish a rapport with the African American males I interviewed so that I could be more authentic and accurate in telling their stories. This meant meeting with these boys and men frequently and for long periods of time. The following table presents the participants, their relationship

Table 1. Frequency of Interviews Conducted

Family	Relationship	Number of Visits	Number of Interviews	Approximate Length of Interviews (Total Time)
The Andersons:				
Charles	Father	4	3	180 minutes
Shaun	Son	4	2	120 minutes
Jeremy	Son	4	3	180 minutes
James	Cousin	2	2	120 minutes
The Wallaces:				
Martin	Father	4	3	180 minutes
Tyreek	Son	3	3	180 minutes
Malik	Cousin	2	2	120 minutes
The Freemans:				
Joshua	Father	3	3	180 minutes
Tyrone	Son	3	3	180 minutes
Jacob	Great-grandfather	2	2	120 minutes
Larry	Cousin	2	2	120 minutes

to each other, the number of times we met, and the length of the interviews we had together.

Finally, as often occurs in qualitative research, participant observation and in-depth interviewing are combined when conducting naturalistic research (Bogdan & Biklen, 2003; Wolcott, 2001). Thus, there is never an interview without observation. Through detailed, written descriptions of the observations made after the interview sessions with my participants, I gained a greater understanding of the contextual and relational factors at work (Ely et al., 1997; Lofland & Lofland, 1995).

Field Notes and Log

Throughout the study, I kept observational notes and interview data in a field log. In an effort to monitor my own bias as a researcher, I maintained this log not only for my transcriptions and descriptions but also for documenting my personal comments, understandings, interpretations, and reflections.

To meet my goal of having a substantive field log, I focused on providing what Geertz (1973) called "thick description." This entailed using the descriptions and transcriptions to highlight areas of significance. In this way, over time my field notes detailed the contexts, relationships, and dynamics of my participants' lives. Furthermore, all the materials in my log were line numbered to make data coding and analysis more efficient. The field log was stored at my home on my computer hard drive and backed up on diskettes. I also kept the electronic copies of my log in a separate location to secure them in the event of any problems with my home computer. The audiocassettes of the interviews were kept in a locked storage cabinet in my home. To further ensure confidentiality, these tape recordings were destroyed in three years.

Analysis Process

The participant observations and qualitative interviews yielded volumes of data, as evident in the participants' rich stories. Strategic steps were taken to carefully understand the emergent themes in the participants' stories, which led to my data analysis. I began the process of data analysis by using the steps Tesch (1990) suggested:

1. I reacquainted myself deeply with my data by selecting and rereading entries from my field log several times.
2. I wrote notes in the margin of these pages about points that interested me and explained why. I also included any insights into topics that came to mind as a result of reading through the data.
3. I then began to make "meaning units" by identifying shifts in meaning within the data (Tesch, 1990).
4. The next step was to create descriptive labels for these meaning units and write them in the margin next to the appropriate lines in the log itself.
5. After repeating these initial steps several times with my log entries, I then comprised a list of these labels and began grouping them together, looking for linkages between the different labels for further analysis.
6. The next step was to analyze the log entries again to see if these labels worked on the data itself. If I found that the labels did not fit with the data, I created new labels to see how they worked with the previously analyzed data.
7. These labels and categories developed from the interview transcripts and observations then assisted me in formulating my major themes.
8. Finally, throughout this process, I wrote analytic memos to capture my insights into and understandings of the categorizing process and analysis.

While I analyzed the data throughout the data collection process, the final comprehensive analysis occurred after the last interview. Throughout the interviewing, I regularly reviewed my field log from beginning to end, not only to familiarize myself with the data but also to support the depth of analysis and meaning-making this research topic required. My early analysis included writing analytic memos and notes within the field log itself, which allowed me to generate further questions and explore initial themes during the data collection. I also periodically brought portions of the data and preliminary findings to the participants for member-checking (Lincoln & Guba, 1989).

Researcher Stance

I came to this study not only as a researcher and a participant in my own family's history, but as an educator. From 1997 to 2003, I was a New York City public-school teacher at a pre-K-8 school with a predominantly African American population. During that time, I grappled with many of the issues that surrounded the education of this group of children, such as a lack of resources, low expectations of students' abilities, and lack of parental involvement. I regularly watched young African American boys being tracked into failure by educational policies that were supposed to help them progress, but were in reality turning them into apathetic and disengaged learners. The years I spent as a classroom teacher only fueled my desire to do research in this area.

As I began to contemplate my study, many questions emerged from my preliminary examination of existing research on African American males. I wondered whether studying African American males across generations would provide a deeper understanding of the complexities of their schooling experiences. How does the culture of the classroom, school, community, and family relate to these young men's educational experiences and professional outcomes? I believe that to make positive and sustainable changes in the schooling experiences and life outcomes of African American males and their families, their voices must be brought to bear on their own problems and successes. In this way, my research sought to explore the qualitative issues that statistical data alone cannot reveal: the actual experiences of African American males in school and in life from their own perspectives and over time. I believe that by listening to and engaging in their stories, we will find ways to positively impact their achievement both inside school and out, giving us ways to redefine, rethink, and ultimately enhance urban education.

Trustworthiness

I employed several strategies to ensure the trustworthiness of my study. First, I separated my personal comments, interpretations, and reflections into observer comments within the log. I also regularly kept analytic memos to capture my insights during the process of collecting, analyzing, and writing. Another strategy was engaging my participants in my collection and analysis processes to maintain the accuracy of my data and findings. My writing and research support group also assisted me in identifying researcher biases and maintaining my trustworthiness. Finally, data from the field log, interviews, and observations were used to identify congruent patterns and themes, as well as to identify any significant data that did not fit into a relevant category. By engaging with the data on these multiple levels, my study moved to producing more dependable results.

31

To further ensure trustworthiness, I also used methods described by Lincoln and Guba (1985), including credibility, transferability, dependability, and confirmability. The first criterion of credibility was established through the writing and research group described above. This group consisted of a team of peers who continually asked questions about my research methods and findings, helping me to remain honest in dealing with the collection and analysis of my data. My efforts to ensure transferability were established by continually striving for "thick" descriptions of my participants and their contexts. In terms of dependability, I thoroughly tracked the shifts in my data and meaning-constructions by closely monitoring my research processes. Finally, confirmability was accomplished when all elements of my data collection and analysis were tracked back to my original sources. Next, Chapter Four presents brief portraits of my participants and background for the analysis that appears in subsequent chapters.

MEET THE FAMILIES

A PROFILE OF THE PARTICIPANTS

Qualitative research is as much about the researcher as it as about those studied (Carothers, 1990). Thus, this chapter reveals my journey in meeting the participants and tracking my own reflections on discovering and rediscovering my connections to and involvement in the African American community. Three families participated in this study: the Andersons, the Wallaces, and the Freemans. All of the families, and the individual members in each family, were given pseudonyms to protect their identities. A total of 11 participants ranging in age from 9 to 73 were interviewed. Of the 11 African American males, three were boys between the ages of 9 and 12. Two participants were biological fathers and one participant was a stepfather. One participant was an older sibling to one of the boys and three participants were cousins in each separate family. One participant was a great-grandfather (see Table 2). The following profiles of each family provide an overview of who they were and how I met them. The next three chapters will then delve more deeply into each of the family's individual stories.

The Andersons

At a reception during a friend's choir performance, I ran into an African American family I had met previously and used this social gathering as an opportunity to seek their participation in my study. The father was immediately receptive and we exchanged numbers, discussing the details of our first official interview.

On the Saturday of our first meeting, I took the subway to the family's home. As I walked the six blocks from the train station, I became a little disoriented and stopped in a bank for cash and much-needed directions. All of the bank's employees were Black or Latino, as were the patrons. I was greeted with a smile and given clear directions to my destination. The environment appeared to be a typical urban area—one that was familiar to me because I grew up in a similar urban area. There was not much foot traffic on the side streets, but the people I encountered were either Black or Latino. It was about 1:30 in the afternoon when I finally arrived on the block where the Andersons lived, identifying the correct side of the street based on the numbers inscribed on the front doors of their brownstone. Adjacent to the Andersons' home was a boarded-up building. As I walked up the steps of their building, I found an empty space where the doorbell should have been. I called the father, letting him know I was waiting outside. A minute later, the front door opened and the smiling face of Shaun, Charles' oldest son, welcomed me into their home.

I followed Shaun inside the brownstone up several flights of stairs to the fourth floor. He directed me to the room where I would find his father. Walking along the mahogany banister, I entered what I thought was a living room and found Charles sitting on the edge of a massive king-size bed. Sitting on a stool between his legs was his youngest son, Jeremy. Charles was braiding Jeremy's long black hair. Just then, Jeremy turned his head in my direction, said hello, and extended his hand to shake mine. I took a seat at the table adjacent to the bed and saw that the only light in the room was coming from the sun radiating through the windows. Its beams shone directly onto Charles' fast-weaving hands and his son's patient face. I was struck by this unusual yet powerful image, one often attributed to African American mothers and daughters, yet it was being so adeptly performed by an African American father for his son. This moment transcended Western notions of gender roles and reminded me of images I have seen countless times of men grooming other men in various parts of Africa. It was the most tender and masculine moment I witnessed throughout my entire study.

Jeremy. Jeremy was a 10-year-old African American fourth grader with a light-brown complexion. He was tall and lean with hazel brown eyes. His long, wavy, black hair was usually pulled back into a thick bushy ponytail or cornrows or braids in long single strands—much like today's Black music artists. He also wore loose jeans and cargo-style pants with T-shirts and a fleece jacket or vest. He told me that he loved to draw, read science fiction books, and play video games and aspired to be an artist when he grew up. He attended a public school in the eastern section of downtown in the City. He said he had a close relationship with his father and experienced typical sibling rivalry with his older brother. That being said, he added that he and his brother were also very supportive of each other.

Shaun. Fourteen-year-old Shaun, a tenth grader, was an African American boy with a complexion close to dark chocolate. He wore his hair in shoulder-length dreadlocks that he usually pulled away from his face into a loose ponytail. He had a winning smile with perfectly straight teeth. He owned the taut cheekbones of a Zulu warrior, yet was very quiet compared with his younger brother, Jeremy. Shaun, like Jeremy, enjoyed school, especially after moving to a new school this past year. He described his old school as just "way too much work and no fun." He was drawn to science and wanted to be physicist when he grew up.

Charles. Charles was a 45-year-old African American man who taught art at the same school his youngest son currently attended. On several occasions, I noticed that he and his youngest child wore similar hairstyles. Charles told me he loved helping children because he believed they were "out-of-the-box thinkers." He was tall, standing over six feet, and shared the same dark-chocolate complexion of his oldest son. He also had long black dreadlocks that ended at the center of his back. With strong chiseled features and a black moustache, Charles had a no-nonsense personality on first impression, but I discovered over time that he was quite a storyteller. He told me that he also loved to cook. Charles was the adoptive father of the boys and was raising them in a single-parent, male-headed household. He explained that at times he was a strict disciplinarian but also was a fun-loving nurturer, depending on the situation.

James. James was Charles' 22-year-old cousin. He had a reddish-caramel complexion with a haircut cut close to his head. Usually, he donned a Muslim-inspired skullcap. He had a faint moustache and a boyish face, and stood about 5'9" tall with a lean and muscular figure. He told me his father was in the U.S. Air Force when he was much younger and he attended a portion of his elementary school years on a military base in Germany before returning to the U.S. He was currently enrolled in a local college and had aspirations of studying business administration.

The Wallaces

I met the Wallaces through a lead from Mr. James, a fifth grade teacher I met at a local community meeting of parents. Once I contacted Martin, the father, he did not hesitate for one moment about being a participant. He asked me to meet him at his job downtown and we would arrange an interview with his son. Throughout the research process, I learned to carry my tape recorder at all times, so having this in tow was perfect when I visited Martin at his office because our first meeting actually turned into an unscheduled interview. After talking for some time, we made an appointment for me to visit the family's home to interview his son, Tyreek.

On the day of our scheduled interview, I took public transportation to the edges of the borough where they lived and found myself once again in the familiar surroundings of my childhood. The housing projects in which the family lived had an intimidating reputation, which was also true of my extended family's neighborhood when I was a young boy. I decided to dress casually that day, wearing a sweatshirt, jeans, sneakers, and a denim jacket. Not wanting to stand out, I put aside my usual interviewing attire of suit and tie. Being raised in such an environment, I knew that residents would know instantly I was an outsider and would treat me as such.

I was a little early—and hungry—so I stopped at the local burger place and grabbed a quick bite. I noticed several White police officers eating in the middle of the dining area, yet the other patrons who were mostly Black and Latino ate on the perimeter and borders of the dining area. As I sat by the front door to eat, I unintentionally caught the attention of a group of teenage girls. I smiled at them and they giggled, tossing their hair behind their shoulders. One girl watched attentively as I took notes in the small, hand-size notebook I had on the table.

When I finished my meal, I walked toward the projects, stopping once on a corner to talk to my sister on my cell phone. Almost immediately, I noticed several cars had slowed down to give me the once-over. I quickly moved a little further into the middle of the block and dropped the hood from my head, letting the rain to pelt my hair. I did not want anyone on either side of the law to think I was up to no good or encroaching on anyone's territory. I ended the call abruptly and crossed the street, ascending the ramp to the entrance of the massive projects—my destination. I kept my head low but my eyes straight ahead as I passed a few older teenagers hanging out in the courtyard.

As I stood by the elevator waiting for its arrival, three small children brushed by me in a race to press the elevator button. A squabble broke out among them and they were completely oblivious to my presence. I thought about their lack of supervision, given that I was never allowed to travel at such a young age without an adult or older sibling. Just then, two young women, probably in their early to mid-twenties and dressed in cropped jeans and colorful blouses, appeared at the elevator pushing strollers. I learned that the playfully loud children were with them when they reprimanded the kids about pressing the elevator button too much. Despite their best efforts, the children did not lower their voices or cease their verbal sparring as we all loaded onto the elevator. I exited first, smiled at them, and said, "Take care." The two women responded similarly as one little boy frowned as he eyed me from behind his dark sunglasses.

Walking down the hallway toward the Wallace's apartment, I saw a young teenage boy up ahead pushing a ten-speed bicycle into the hallway. Based on the apartment letters and spacing of the doors I had already passed, I estimated he was leaving the Wallace's apartment. Just then, another boy around the same age appeared and I could tell from their resemblance that he was Martin's son, Tyreek. He had features almost identical to his father, but his complexion was a few shades darker than Martin's.

Tyreek. Tyreek was an 11-year old African American male, standing about five feet tall. With the shadow of a moustache emerging over his upper lip, Tyreek had metal braces on his teeth and usually wore athletic clothes such as basketball jerseys, becoming a replica of his favorite players with sweatpants and sneakers. Tyreek said he liked school but felt that his current teacher did not seem to like him. Speaking with an affect well beyond his young age, Tyreek told me he was changing schools because he did not like the strict discipline policies of his current school.

Martin. Martin was in his mid-forties and had a light golden complexion and moustache. His wavy black hair showed touches of gray at the temples. Martin was bi-racial, but self-identified as an African American because of his family's roots in the southern United States—specifically his father's family history. Martin liked his job where he trained and helped former parolees find work. He took his occupation seriously and refused several promotions and job offers because he was dedicated to helping former inmates at this pivotal point in their lives. When he was much younger, he was arrested and spent two years in prison for what he referred to as "a not-so-smart decision." Now, he used his own experiences in life and those of the people he helped as fodder to inspire his son, Tyreek, to avoid similar pitfalls.

Malik.   Malik was Tyreek's 14-year-old cousin. He lived with his mother in the same building and often came to visit the Wallaces. He told me that he spent nearly every day hanging out with Tyreek. When he could not stop by to see the Wallaces, he at least tried to call. Malik was in eighth grade and attending the same school that Tyreek intended to transfer to next year for the sixth grade. Malik said that he loved playing computer games and wanted to design them with Tyreek when they got older.

The Freemans

I met the last family, the Freemans, through word-of-mouth or by what sociologists call "snowball sampling" (Heckathorn, 1997). A friend of a family member told me she knew of a family who would be interested in participating in my study. Soon after, my friend gave me a telephone number to contact them. My connection began after speaking to Tyrone's grandmother, Lucille, on the telephone, explaining the details of my study. Lucille's verbal enthusiasm convinced me she would definitely solidify the participation of her son Joshua and her step-grandson Tyrone. Without even speaking with either one, she went as far as setting up a time and date for my first meeting with Joshua and his stepson, Tyrone, at her apartment outside the City. All of my interviews took place at Lucille's apartment where her son Joshua grew up in—again in the projects where three of their generations had lived.

These were the very same projects I had come to as a child when my family visited our extended relatives. I wish I could say I had completely fond memories of visiting these projects but I do not. I remember teenagers hanging out and smoking in the courtyards, music blasting from boom boxes, folks yelling up to windows screaming to be buzzed in the front doors of the buildings, garbage occasionally being tossed from windows to the streets below. As I grew older, I remember evenings filled with gunshots and the stories adults told of people being mugged in the neighborhood. These images ran counter to what I experienced once inside the safe confines of my relatives' home. Here, I remember hearing laughter, eating good food, playing board games, watching Bugs Bunny and Daffy Duck cartoons, and dancing with my older cousins to the latest jams on the radio.

From the street, the buildings looked exactly the same as they did on my last visit over 20 years ago—just a little more worn down. The courtyard was empty, and as I passed two Black men dressed in flight bomber jackets, sneakers, and baseball hats, I overheard one say to the other, "That's Amar's cousin." Not completely sure I had heard them correctly; I decided not to make eye contact with them. I still have family living in these projects and can only assume that the young man's comment could be attributed to my letting my own relatives know I was coming to interview the Freemans and would stop by to see them when I was done. I remember the "code" of the projects when I was child to let people know when a "known" stranger or relation was around. I guess in this way my family always looked after my relatives and me when we came to visit. Perhaps this young man saw the strong family resemblance my family members share.

After trying the intercom by the door and getting no response, I waited for someone to exit the building so I could enter. An older Latino male in his mid-fifties, a woman, and a very young girl with long black hair pulled back in a ponytail entered the building with me. I stepped out of the way to let them in by holding the door open. The man smiled at me approvingly and said, "Thank you." He then held the elevator door open for me and I thanked him. Suddenly, I was overtaken by a familiar stench of urine in the elevator—bringing me back to my childhood visits. When I looked down, I saw a dried yellow stain by the metal drain at the center of the elevator. I learned as a child that some men would urinate in elevators either because they were too drunk or just too angry—"They're mad at the world," my mother would often say. I remember always wondering if their anger at the world actually fueled this behavior or if they were just using poor judgment.

As the elevator door opened to my floor, I moved forward and said, "Have a good night" to my elevator companions. When I stepped off the metal contraption, I noticed thick glass bricks in the main corridor. As a young boy, I remembered pressing my face against one of those bricks, trying to see through their ribbed thickness to the other side. All I could see was a distorted carnival-mirror view of my own face reflecting back. I wondered metaphorically how this daily distortion impacted the lives of my participants.

I knocked on the door of the family's apartment and was immediately welcomed in by Lucille, Joshua's mother. I could tell by her greeting that it had really helped to make this connection through a family friend. The apartment was laid out very differently than my own family's apartment: it was a railroad-style apartment with long, narrow hallways. This apartment was also much boxier, and I wondered how the huge wraparound black leather sofa in the living room had been maneuvered in through the small front door. Lucille told me to take a seat at the kitchen table and offered me something to drink. I asked for water and she made me some hot tea, of her own volition; I thanked her profusely.

She told me that her son, Joshua, was running a little late and would arrive in about 20 minutes. In the interim, we talked about my research and she praised its importance. Seemingly out of the blue, she announced that Joshua was home. I wondered how she knew, but then I heard a little jingling sound seconds before the front door opened. Both Joshua and Tyrone entered. Joshua smiled and shook my hand and told me I looked like my cousins. He nudged Tyrone a bit and he grunted a quick greeting. Typical of a boy his age from this neighborhood, Tyrone muttered "S'up." Lucille corrected him, instructing him to say, "Hello. How are you?" Or "Nice to meet you."

Tyrone gave me all three greetings one after the other and then smiled proudly. Lucille nodded her head approvingly and then looked at Tyrone, suddenly shouting,

"Come here, boy, and give me some sugar!" Tyrone flew to her side and kissed her on the cheek. She asked him how school was while gently removing his baseball cap from his head. She then said to us all, "Let me get out the way so you can talk."

Father Joshua and his stepson Tyrone sat down with me at the kitchen table and I began to explain the purposes of my study.

Tyrone. Tyrone was a 10-year-old African American boy with a tawny-brown complexion and quick smile. He had brown eyes and low-cut hair like his father. Tyrone told me he did not like school but enjoyed art classes. He said he did not read much anymore. He also said he had an older brother whom his parents felt did not provide the best example for him to emulate. Tyrone added he liked sports and computer games. According to his mother and stepfather, he was good in math, but recently his grades started to slip. He had a special relationship with his stepfather, Joshua, since his biological father was not a part of his life.

Joshua. Joshua was 23 years old and had a biological daughter with Tyrone's mother. Joshua grew up with what he described as "the pull of the streets" for his entire life. He was about 6'3" with a hefty, solid frame. His eyes were hazel brown like his "Grandpa Jacob's." He had an easy smile and his hazel eyes twinkled as he talked about his childhood and spending time with his grandfather Jacob at family gatherings. He told me he was almost incarcerated as a teenager for attempting to sell drugs on the streets of his neighborhood. He also said he had a close relationship with his younger sister, Maxine, who lived with their mother, Lucille, in the same apartment. While he usually had a deep voice that boomed at times; his voice also tended at times to trail off to a whisper. He went to the local neighborhood schools and eventually graduated from high school. He said he wanted to go to college for either education or business administration.

Larry. Larry, Joshua's cousin, was 22 years old, standing at about 5'10" and speaking with a mild southern accent. He had sparkling white teeth and close-cropped hair. Joshua and Larry spent time together as children in the South and still kept in contact from time to time. Larry told me he was trying to inspire Joshua to go to college and live out his dreams. When I interviewed Larry, he had just graduated from college and was contemplating graduate school in his future. He has his own car and was close to his own father. In our meeting, he told me he was adjusting to being home after college and was looking for a job.

Jacob. A tall man standing at 6'2", Jacob was in his early seventies and currently lived in a quaint southern town with his second wife. He was Joshua's grandfather and Tyrone's great-grandfather. He was in good physical condition and walked and exercised regularly with his friends. He had a light-caramel complexion with curly salt and pepper hair and hazel-brown eyes. Jacob said he attributed the color of his skin and eyes to his great-grandfather who also had darker skin and green eyes.

Jacob worked as a truck driver for many years for a shipping company, but now was retired and living in the South. Jacob said he visited his family in the North a few times a year and they too came to visit him on major holidays such as Christmas and Thanksgiving. Jacob said he was very active in his church and described himself as a "deep thinker" who always took his time responding to questions.

Table 2 serves as a reminder of who the participants are, their relationship to each other, their age, level of education, and current occupation.

Table 2. Study Participants

Family	Relationship	Age	Education	Occupation
The Andersons:				
Charles	Father	45	Master's degree	Art teacher
Shaun	Son	14	10th grade	Student
Jeremy	Son	10	4th grade	Student
James	Charles' cousin	19	College freshman	Student
The Wallaces:				
Martin	Father	48	1 year of college	Project manager
Tyreek	Son	11	5th grade	Student
Malik	Tyreek's cousin	14	8th grade	Student
The Freemans:				
Joshua	Step-father	23	High school graduate	Store clerk
Tyrone	Step-son	10	4th grade	Student
Jacob	Tyrone's great-grandfather	73	High school graduate	Retired
Larry	Joshua's cousin	22	College graduate	Office assistant

MEET THE ANDERSONS

My childhood was great, I was always surrounded by family, my mother, my brothers, sisters, aunts, uncles, and cousins—we did everything together.

-Family as described by Charles Anderson

Charles Anderson was the single father of two adopted sons, Jeremy and Shaun. They lived in a historically Black community. I visited the family four times at their home over a six-month period and spent approximately three to four hours per visit. I conducted three interviews with Jeremy and Charles and two with Shaun and James; each interview lasted 45 to 60 minutes. I noticed that over time the members of the family seemed to become more relaxed with my presence in their home. They often asked each other questions and engaged in side conversations during the interviews. Also by the second interview there was an expectation that I would stay for a home-cooked meal or just spend some time engaging in conversation once the day's interviews were completed.

DISCUSSION OF THE ANDERSONS

The narrative accounts from the members of the Anderson family revealed an insightful journey of a family of African American males. Their experiences were varied and nuanced, with both positive and negative schooling experiences that appeared across generations. Some of these experiences happened inside their classrooms, while others occurred outside of the schools in their home communities. They discussed the challenging aspects of being African American males in

Table 3. Anderson Family Overview

Family	Relationship	Age	Education	Occupation
ANDERSON:				
Charles	Father	45	MS Degree	Art Teacher
Shaun	Son	14	10th grade	Student
Jeremy	Son	10	4th grade	Student
James	Cousin	19	College Freshman	Student

yesterday's and today's educational contexts—from the father's experiences of urban school desegregation in the 1970s, to one son's experience with teachers that may not have been very culturally responsive with their disciplinary decisions. Still, we had an older brother who enjoyed school, was self-motivated, and held high expectations for his future; moreover, he had positive interactions with his teachers and his peers. Then we had the father's cousin who was self-motivated but also keenly aware of the racism and discrimination for which he was on the receiving end because he was an African American male. He also dis cussed the educational shifts within his own family.

Through Charles' story, we are made aware of the influence of a strong mother, despite an absent father, and her emphasis on the importance of education became the educational vision that continued to be passed on to this group of males in this family. This vision of the value of education was imparted to this father who then passed it on to his sons. In his cousin's immediate family, we learn of the struggles of a supportive yet under-educated father who, despite his own academic shortcomings, instilled the value of education in his son. Thirty-six years separated the elder father, Charles, from his youngest son, Jeremy. What did they say about their schooling experiences across the decades? In their own words, hear the Anderson's stories.

Jeremy the Son: A 10-year-old Fourth Grader

Jeremy was a young African American male who appeared very comfortable in whom he was both inside and outside of school. He credited much of this to the influence of his father Charles, who was present in both of the important spaces in his young life—home and school.

When I asked Jeremy how he felt about school, he responded by sharing how his father asked him to communicate the details of any situation in which he got into trouble at school:

> For me school is just regular, I don't care about it sometimes. Yeah, I like school, but the thing is if I like get into big trouble my teacher can just go downstairs and like call my dad. Whenever I get into trouble I do letters, I write letters to my dad and he asks why. He asks me to explain everything. My teacher, sometimes she gets mad and doesn't want to talk. Like on Friday me and my friend, we were playing kickball and we collided and he started screaming at me 'cause he thought I was in his territory. And I called him a jerk and my teacher she didn't like let me speak.

As Jeremy further explained what he liked about school, he also gave an example of the frustration he felt with his current teacher:

> She just went with him because he was crying. I didn't feel really bad, but not really good either, 'cause she does that a lot. She does that with everyone in the class. We used to do highs and lows in school. From 0 to +5 is high, from

0 to -5 is low—it means you're having a bad day. Then we sit around and talk about it. It's a chart with our names on it and we get to move where we are to show how we feel that day. You can move it anytime when we're about to do something else. Yeah, transitioning. I don't move it anymore, no one does. Now it's in the box where we keep the names. We barely even remember what that thing was. Like when I really start something, and then she'll go and not do it anymore and nobody does it. Like we have this book thingy, and we're supposed to write the number of books that we've read and nobody does *that* anymore. We just write about books in our reading notebooks.

Jeremy shared the details of what he was currently doing in art and reading, which were two of his favorite subjects:

One of the good things that I like about school is art. So now we have partners every week and we do like self-portraits of our partners. Like the first day we were drawing our shoes. I drew those in the picture hanging on the wall in the living room and everyone at school wanted it. I started drawing when I was really, really, really, really young! I like to draw comics. I also like math and reading, too. I love to read. I can read like ten books in a month. I read a lot. I read all three *Lord of the Rings* books…in a week, that's like three thousand pages long. I have a favorite book called *Eragon* and I have a favorite author, her name is Anna Devere Smith. I read her book, *Letters to a Young Artist*, it was interesting. I write, but just weird stuff, like I'm the king of the world. I don't know, like I try to draw and write first thing in the morning. But sometimes I'm tired and I'll just wait until my brother gets ready.

Jeremy talked about how his family supported him with his work outside of school. His brother did not really help him with his schoolwork. His father was the one in the family who helped him with his homework. He described his father as "fun and energetic." In speaking of his favorite subjects and his teachers, Jeremy shed light on the discontinuity between his favorite space to be in at school and his least favorite teacher:

One of my favorite subjects and it's not really a favorite, 'cause I don't really like the librarian, but I like to do the library. I like to get on the computers. Sometimes we get extra time to play games on the computer. But I don't like the librarian. She's mean! One time me and my friend, were playing around and she said she's going to hang us from a tree! It was upsetting. It was weird… she tells kids a lot of things like: she'll take out a gun and shoot you…she says that to the whole class. I told my dad and he spoke to the principal. The lady who's the librarian was my first grade teacher. She always used to scream at me 'cause she didn't want me to talk while she was talking. The only thing that changed about her is her hair color.

This memory was juxtaposed with a positive memory he had about his first teacher and the impact of his father being a teacher at the school he currently attended. He recalled making cookies with his first teacher and meeting her husband. About his father being a teacher at his school, he saw it as a "mixed blessing" because if he got into trouble of any kind, his teachers could tell his father right away. On the other hand, when he needed advice, his father was close by. In sharing the best and worst things that had happened to him in school, he began with a comment on what he felt his school lacked in resources:

> My school needs more computers and new books 'cause the books we have are boring. I ask my teacher to recommend a book for me to read sometimes. The worst thing that happened in school was that librarian thing. The best...I can only remember things that happened outside of school—like Camp Days in June, when we go all day to the park and the only time we come back is for lunch. We play all day.

Charles the Father: A 45-year-old Art Teacher

Charles' story provides insight into the important role he played in the continuing development of both of his sons' lives. He was an inspirational role model for his youngest son, Jeremy, and his presence was clearly felt both in school and at home. He taught art at Jeremy's school and enjoyed being a father to his two sons. He made sure that the family spent quality time together each day—this was a tradition he drew from his own childhood experiences with his mother and siblings.

Charles spoke of his earliest memories of school and, specifically in our initial interview, of his art teacher who imposed restrictions on him and his classmates:

> I went to public school in an outer borough, pre-K to 3 and a different public school in another borough from third to sixth grade. Elementary school was great; I went to a public school that was right down the street from my house. It was literally a half a block away. It was a charter school; it was one of the oldest schools in the borough. It's no longer there; they tore it down when I was in seventh grade. I remember it was one of those old, old buildings, I remember it, it was one of those with the desks stuck to the floor. Yes, they were bolted to the floor. I remember my art class. I remember my art teacher; she gave a kid a Rex-O from a coloring book. She gave each kid the same Rex-O. She would give you little pieces of carbonation. She would give you one pencil, then she gave each kid one crayon. It was from those boxes with eight colors. Yeah, you got to pick the color you want and that's how green became my favorite color. Then you have to raise your hand and go, "Excuse me Miss Duchess, may I have another crayon, another color crayon, please?" And she would go, "Yes, you may." And you would color your little blue spot. I remember you had to be vary careful about what color you chose because by the time she got back to you, you had to just sit there and wait. I remember thinking I better not pick that color for that Black spot. I'd pick the largest part to color green. Yeah, and that's what we did for the whole forty-five minutes and that was art class.

As the conversation quickly shifted to his memories of high school in the early 1970s, the impact of being bused to school at the time of school desegregation became the focus. Charles remembered what it was like at that time being bused to a school in a White neighborhood. According to him, for the first six months of school, all of the White students picketed outside the school building. Charles said, "They were chanting 'Neighborhood schools for neighborhood children!" He also shared how this was on the television news for a length of time. His mother watched while he was commuting home from school and relayed to him what the news story reported.

In interviewing Charles over time, I later learned about his experiences as a single father raising African American boys. Charles explained:

The hardest part for me being a single parent raising two boys is saying what you mean, meaning what you say, and keeping your ground. Being a single parent or just a parent period is hard. I remember my friend told me that when I become a parent, I will understand what she's going through because at the time, she was a single parent of an eight-year-old. I remember one time she and I were standing at the corner waiting to cross the street and there were no cars. I just looked at her like she was crazy and said why don't we cross the street. She would not move until the light turned green and it was just her and I. She said when you become a parent, you'll understand why. And now I do. There are things you do as a person without children that you don't think about like jaywalking. I always cook dinner—even if we eat dinner out. There always has to be something for them to eat. My mother would leave for work when I was a child and I remember we ate dinner at 3:30. Once we were done and the dishes were in the sink, then she'd say, "Okay, guys, I'm going to work." I guess that always just stuck with me.

Charles provided in-depth insight about how he supported his children and his expectations for their futures. He called his honesty and clarity of expectations the tools he employed to support his sons successfully. As he responded, he offered his personal philosophy about the concept of graduation. Charles did not believe children "graduate until high school"; everything prior to this he considers transitioning forward or "moving on." He always made sure to answer any questions they had about school and what to expect as they progressed through school. Charles discussed the importance of making positive choices in one's life and the influence of having friends who inspire one to continue making progress:

I talk to them about college all the time. You know you'll watch TV and see people who didn't go to college and I'll say some people chose to not go to college. But these are the two choices and this is the road that not going to college leads and this is the road that going to college will lead to. I said when I was growing up no one really talked to me about college per se, but they talked about the importance of school and getting as much education that I can get. I had friends who talked about college. Part of my success as a father is remembering the mistakes I made when I was a kid. I love being a father. It's scary, but I can see their future clear as day. I knew what they were going to do when they were little.

The dynamics were slightly different now for his oldest son, Shaun, now that he had moved to a different school. He discussed how his father continued to build that bridge between home and school.

Shaun the Brother: A 14-year-old Tenth Grader

Shaun appeared to be listening closely to his father's advice as he moved forward through school. He gave much thought to several issues regarding his schooling as a young African American male and his future. Shaun told me what came to mind when he thought about school:

> I like school because I like learning and hanging with my friends. Going to school is fun because I'm with friends and I'm also learning. Yeah, well it depends. It feels like it's kind of hard and then it feels like it's normal. Like it's easy. The hardest year of high school is the first and then it's like about adjusting to that high school life in three years left. So once you get into the tenth grade, it's easier adjusting to that high school life. Schoolwork comes easier, you know what to expect, especially if you've been in that school the previous year.

As he talked about what he liked, Shaun also described the challenges he faced, particularly in middle school:

> My middle school was a very hard school, it was a K through 12 school and it was really hard. Like you'd come home and have five hours worth of homework a night. Some nights I'd be up until like 1 o'clock and still doing homework and I started homework at 4 o'clock. But now it's like, but now I get home from school at like 4:15 every day except on Mondays because I have basketball, but now I'm done with homework at like 6 o'clock and sometimes even sooner. Elementary school was basically the same, like being with a bunch of friends, getting to know people, and just being very social. That's like to me a major part of school. I guess what was challenging sometimes was trying to pass the state and citywide tests. Well, my teachers really, really cared for me. They took the time out, like there were after-school programs. For example, if there was a city-wide test, they would start test-prep two months in advance and that would be a couple days after school and that would help you, and stuff like that, prepare you for the test. I didn't really have any major problems at school when I was younger. I get along with everybody.

We conversed about his supports at home and if his father talked to him about school. Shaun mentioned how his father discussed his own school experiences with him now that he was in high school. Shaun saw these conversations as helping him deal with high school and prepare for college. He talked about how in his advisory period at school they discussed other options besides college as well. He saw a clear connection between what he heard at home and in school. Shaun offered this description of the close relationship that his father and teachers had established:

> Yeah, my dad and my teachers, they talk. Like sometimes, like last year my dad and my English teacher they talked a lot. They're on a first name basis. Actually, I have to call my teachers by their last name and they're on a first name basis so they talk a lot. I really don't care.

Shaun provided further details about the trouble he was having in English and how his father and his teacher supported him:

> Well, English, it's kind of hard, well, basically it depends on what we are studying. Well, I had a little trouble in English in the ninth grade, then in tenth grade because we mostly…I was adjusting to high school, to ninth grade English and last year we studied Greek word roots, and that was kind of hard. And it was just getting myself to sit down and do the work, which was kind of hard too. I just couldn't do it. Well, my English teacher kept calling the house and she kept calling the house and talking to my father and they just really clicked. They bonded like this (snaps fingers twice). Well, I acted the same way I usually did in class, I'm just energetic. It wasn't a matter that it was my behavior and I wasn't being good and stuff like that. It was just that I wouldn't hand in my work. I wouldn't do it. Like I talk to everybody, including the teachers. Like the teachers are kind of the same way too.

Shaun smiled as he talked about his relationship with his peers at school. "My friends," he said, "well, they're kind of just like me, they're friends, they're there for me, we joke around a lot." Like him, his friends liked to play sports. He suggested that "Some of the girls are better than the boys at football." Shaun talked about his plans for the future and what he wanted to do professionally when he finished school. He claimed to be interested in becoming a forensic specialist or a crime-scene investigator. At the time, he still had not officially decided what he wanted to do later in life.

Shaun explained the unique way he found out about his younger brother's problems when Jeremy talked in his sleep:

> I'm four years older than my brother. He wants to be an artist. Sometimes we'll talk about his experiences in school. Well, like we don't really intentionally talk, like sometimes it will just come out like he'll end up saying it. And but really he goes to my father, not me. Like whatever goes on during the day, he'll like say whatever. Like sometimes when he doesn't say something during the day it will come out when he's sleeping because he talks in his sleep. And then I'll just ask him about it. And once the conversation is over, then we just go

about our business. Like sometimes he'll be like I was just talking to my friends or I was just saying this and this. And then I'll offer some suggestions—but it just depends on what it is.

In a conversation about why he thought large groups of African American males were not doing well in school, Shaun exclaimed:

Basically, I think some of them it's about just sitting down and just doing the work. And not just going home and jumping right on the computer and hanging out outside and stuff like that. They don't want to sit down and don't want to do their work. Or they do their work at the last minute, so their grades won't be as high. But then again some people do their work at the last minute and their grades are higher. They actually might take a whole week to write an essay, they might get lower than just doing it that day before. Maybe they're not going to the teacher to ask for some help. And maybe there's a teacher that they don't like and they probably want to disrespect the teacher and act up, the teacher may not like them because they're giving them attitude maybe. I would say it depends. Like a teacher can show it, like if there's something they really don't like you doing they can show it in a facial expression. The only other thing that I would probably have seen or heard about is they call home all the time and call the parents. Yeah. Like they'll sit down with you one on one.

Shaun followed up with a positive example of the support he received from one of his teachers:

We were on a trip and we were on the train. I was sitting with four of my friends and the English teacher came over and she told each one of the students, one person is not handing in a research paper, this person is not doing their homework, and the other person is not doing this. And I noticed that she was talking to everyone around me and then she said and you, I congratulate you. Like she'll tell if you've done something good and you've done your work. Right, good news for you but the rest of you, you haven't handed in this or that. Well, I guess they were kind of embarrassed and the train was crowded, so there were definitely a whole lot of people listening. I felt good 'cause there were people standing around listening, so that other people in the world would know. No, because like nobody really care, 'cause if you do your work, you do your work; if you don't do your work, you don't do your work. 'Cause that really doesn't have any effect on other people. 'Cause if you did your work, you do your work; if you don't do your work, then that's on you. I guess they were just angry about a bad grade or something.

James the Cousin: A 21-year-old Graduate Student

While Shaun was a 14-year-old in this family thinking about many issues, his 21-year-old cousin, James, who spent a large amount of time with family, offered additional perspectives. For James, as well as the other members of the Anderson family, the social and emotional support they received from their families helped to inform the linkages to their academic success. James recalled his childhood and his earliest memories of school:

> I'm in graduate school at college in the city. I always thought school was fun. My early memories of school are a lot of participation, cooperation, I remember kindergarten and first grade. Of course, where you did napping and then of course, recess. But it was always a lot of games, um, interactive games. I did kindergarten and first grade in a different country, Germany, from five to ten years old. So, um they had a language, not courses, but language participation or interaction. I was born here.

James talked about the challenges he faced developing friends at school in Germany. He had a friend at the time who he could only communicate with in German. For James, the culture in Germany was very different than what he was used to. His father was in the military and the family followed him wherever he was stationed. American culture was still prevalent because these were American bases and everyone spoke English. James said, "My earliest years I remember close friendships, kinships… the friendships I developed in my early years had nothing to do with academia. It was more social." He was shy as a child and did not feel the need to engage in after-school programs:

> When I came back here, school was the same structure here as there. You had five or six periods, you had a recess, you had lunch. You had after-school activities which I never took part in. Because I had my own hobbies at home I liked to do and be like involved with myself. And plus my parents never really cared…my mom was home after school. Somebody was always home, so they never had a reason to send me off to after-school camps or anything like that. I didn't miss out on anything because I didn't go, I mean it was just playing… ball! Basically, the same things I would do at home, so it was no big deal…not for me. I was kind of shy anyway. So my observations were more inward than outward. I was paying more attention to myself than I was to everybody else. 'Cause I always felt so different. Everyone else was always able to express themselves openly, I was more quiet.

In talking with this 21-year-old, I could see he had much to say about many different topics. On the media's representation of young Black males and its influence on society's perception of them; James said:

> Well, it's a point of view thing…what I see in terms of media, advertising, newspapers, what have you. It just seems like the average young Black male is supposed to be selling drugs on the corner mainly in this city or most urban areas. Supposed to be selling drugs on the corner, um might be slightly educated, but just street education. Know how to count money, know how to

count drugs. Know how to add this up and add that up. Um, supposed to have at least two or three kids by the age of twenty-five, thirty. Supposed to have at least done maybe three or four years in prison. Have done a prison term… hmm. Supposed to dress like everybody else and have their clothes hanging off and if you don't then you're a nerd. At least that's how I see it. And my experience in this city has been that. People…my peers, like different areas that I've lived in they see and they think automatically—I'm one of their *exact* peers, I'm supposed to be on the corner selling drugs.

James had a serious reaction to his not fitting into people's stereotypes. He shared how he could never see himself succumbing to the lure of illegal activities like selling drugs, or negative activities typically associated with urban African American males his age:

When they find out I'm more involved in…other things, then…it's almost like…I'm either absolutely strange to them or they just don't know what to make of me. How I deal with it, I…I'm just who I am. I can't change them; um…what I do is I don't let it really bother me. I know I'm not fit to be on the streets, on the corner selling drugs…'cause I'll be dead. I mean it's just not the kind of life that I grew up with. Um, I grew up around it, uh, but I was never part of it. So I wouldn't know the first thing about greeting people and figuring out, oh well, this person wants this. I don't know it's just not *my thing* as they say. Oh, I just kept myself separate from it when necessary.

For some of James' cousins, this was not the case, as he commented:

I had cousins that I was very close to, so we did a lot of things together, but when push came to shove, when it came to being around them or they were at this spot I would just have to go somewhere else because my grandma would kill me! School was basically nonexistent, they didn't care. I mean it was just like another day. It wasn't a big issue to graduate, to finish high school, to go on to college. It wasn't a big issue for them. They was just….well, one cousin in particular that I'm thinking about. We're the exact same age, we did everything together, we grew up together…he never really cared about school. The only reason he went to school was for the girls, and so he wouldn't have to sit at home all day, doing nothing and watch paint dry.

James elaborated further about segregation in the past and segregated schools today. He offered insights on the issues that young Black students face in society:

Well, I don't think it was anything inside school besides the fact that the school was very segregated, 'cause it's in the South. Things are still very segregated there and growing up it was very evident. So, but I don't think…that, it's such an everyday part of life. You don't really pay attention to it as much. It affects you greatly, but you don't pay attention to how it affects you or that it affects you. You just live with it and say, oh well, hey, it is what it is. With that being said, I think that uh, even, I'm speaking for him, which might not be as safe as speaking to him directly. I think it was the outside. Growing up in the ghetto, having to struggle. Seeing your parents struggle, see your mother struggle, see your family struggle, to scrape this up and scrape that up. And it became pressure just being young and being Black, growing up, I want to say America; I want to say the South. But I'm not sure what the context of...all I can say right now is being young and Black. Society would have you believe that there's not many options out there for you. You know you watch movies, you watch TV, you hear things people say. I mean there's a multitude of people that don't want to see you do well. Why, I'm not sure, I mean they have their own insecurities.

In describing his relationship with some of his former teachers, James recalled a negative incident with one teacher in particular:

I remember my tenth grade in high school I had this teacher and she hated me. She never showed me she hated me, she was always very pleasant towards me. But certain things she said and certain things she did. I would write my papers, put my all into my papers and I would still flunk. Oh, she would tell me I'm "too grandiose, I want to use big words when there's no necessity for me to use them." What I was trying to *do* was not to, just trying to be comfortable knowing what the words meant and to be able to use them. Which apparently she wasn't teaching me. So she would read my papers and say, "Oh, well, this word is too grandiose, you should think simply." She used to always tell me think more simply. In other words, words like cat...dog, you know. She hated me! I think as a young Black male, I was giving her more than she was used to seeing. She wasn't used to seeing somebody so ambitious, so passionate about *school*.

James believed this teacher's actions were based on her own insecurities about empowering him with knowledge. About teachers and teaching, he added:

What I do know is that a teacher should deal with students equally and be the mediator between the student and their success in the future. And what they know, their knowledge base, their expectations, basically that's what I'm trying to say. I don't think she saw me anymore than...mm, I wouldn't say a janitor, I think she revered me a little bit more than that, but not much. Maybe a mechanic or a carpenter, she used to always tell me I should be good with my hands. Yeah, even though I never, I never did anything to prove to her that I am good with my hands. That is, I never made a papier-mâché animal or something for her, she just thought I would be better off with a hands-on trade.

James concluded with how he made meaning of the acts of teachers:

Like I said, I was kind of shy, so I didn't consult with other students and say, "Well, what is she saying to you?" I just took it in and I mean...all right, I've never had more than two or three Black males in my classes all my life. So, um, I noticed, well, she didn't like them. She hated me particularly. They didn't have much and they weren't really ambitious. They just did their papers and turned them in. Whatever grade she gave they were content with. So I did notice when certain other students came to her, particularly the White students, her demeanor just changed. All of a sudden she was more inviting, she was more...ah, like she wanted to deal with them and help teach them, you know.

When I probed into his other teachers, James discussed them in relation to how he viewed his cousin, but also shared another negative incident that he recently experienced with one of his teachers:

My other teachers were much like Charles'. They had their lives. Just fun loving, free-spirited, didn't care who you were as long as you had an ambition to learn; it was almost like they don't see color. They don't let that become the barrier of their decision or the basis of their decision. Um, another White teacher same year, same semester, same grade, she was my English teacher. And she, she liked me and she would help me: Well, you don't want to use this word, you want to say this, give me synonyms" and so...I guess I got both ends of the bargain.

For James, discrimination extended beyond the color line. He talked about discrimination he received from a Chinese professor in one of his graduate courses. He described the situation and how he handled it when confronted with the discriminatory actions of one of his recent teachers; he decided to take action:

So one day she pulls me aside and says, "Based on your responses in class, I don't think that you're going to make it out of this class with a passing grade." And she also told me, "I see the same thing in other students, a few other students in the class." But she wouldn't say who they are, she wouldn't say anything about it, but that's where she left it. Oh, I don't know. I was the only Black American there. I mean there are other Blacks there, but they're from different countries, African, people from Haiti, Indians, Chinese. Well, if she says what's $2 + 2$, and I raise my hand and I say 5. Even though that's not how it went. She's basing it on my response to her in class, teaching at the board. Which I think is wrong. I remember, a couple of times, she asked outright, "What do you do with this graph?" and I went up and I showed her and I got no credit for that. But she heard whatever mistake I had in class, like linear equations. I want to tell her about herself. Part of me wants to, but by the same token, she could be helping me in saving me time. If she going to flunk me, it doesn't make sense to keep sitting there in her class, if she's already told me she's going to fail me. I didn't go to her; I went to her boss.

James reflected on the quality of support he received in the past from his family around his education. He explained how he received very little support from his mother with school, while the bulk of the support came from his father:

They really didn't know my mother, nobody ever knew my mom. She was there; she just wasn't active in it. She had her own life, she was sewing, knitting and doing ceramics and crafts and all that kind of stuff. Well, I've always felt that when people strike up conversations about their father not being there, I can't really contribute a great deal because my dad has always been there. Even though we've had our ups and downs. Even when my mom wasn't there, my father has always been there. So I don't know what it means not to have a positive Black male role model. Yeah, I think so because he's always been very supportive of me, even when I don't do well. You know, I bring home a grade that's not satisfactory. You know, he offers moral support. If I got a B, he's like "Well, you didn't get an A." He's happy for the B. He'll give me a couple of dollars, you know, five dollars or something. You know you still could have got an A, right? You know, don't be so lazy next time.

About the education of males in his family and what he knew of their experiences, James reported:

I knew that my father dropped out. He didn't finish high school. He joined the military, um, when he was young, about eighteen, nineteen. He didn't finish high school. He didn't graduate from high school, but he did finish up to like the ninth, tenth grade. He did some college but he never completed any college. He did some, just a couple courses here and there through the military. I mean he's spoken to me about that, but me and my brothers, as a matter of fact my whole generation, are the first ones to officially go to school, to officially receive degrees. Everybody else has training vocational, you know, mechanical, just different technical training, but no degrees; nobody has degrees. Um, I think our parents were focused on growing healthy children and making sure that their children ate. Had a place to sleep everyday and had clothes on their back. Um, that was more important to them…than getting an education. They couldn't do both, I mean seven or eight kids—they couldn't do both.

James talked about how his brothers were not really involved in his academic life:

I have two brothers and no sisters. I'm the middle child. My oldest brother, he's three years older than me. Let's see, he's in the air force for eleven years now. Married, two kids. My younger brother, uhhhh, sad to say he's under house arrest right now for dealin' drugs. He's gone the other route, it's typical, you know, it's either/or. My relationship with my older brother…none really, 'cause we really weren't raised together. We spent time together up until about twelve, my age, up until about twelve, thirteen and after that he went off and lived with my aunts, went to college. And then joined the military. So after that we really didn't grow together, I don't know him like that. Yeah…he couldn't help me! You know, I mean the classes I took were a little too advanced for him. 'Cause he was never really…I think he had it, but he didn't care to use it. He was more like basketball, history, those types of things were his subjects. Math and science never has been…what I'm interested in.

James' younger brother was dealing with the repercussions of choosing an illegal lifestyle of selling drugs and their relationship suffered as a result. James believed that his brother was "babied too much by my mother":

My younger brother is eight years younger than me and he grew up without my father. He grew up with my mother. My own personal opinion is that he was spoonfed everything, so he doesn't know how to take care of his self. He doesn't know how to think for his self. Um, he got too much. Yeah, I was around. But not really, not really. They couldn't help him with school. It's not that they couldn't—they didn't help him with school, they just didn't. Um, they were more involved with did he eat today, is he okay. Um, you know, we're talking about people who still have a mind frame of the Fifties and the Sixties and back in the day where an education was not what it is today, you know. I don't know, somehow he was influenced by the streets and they became his family. And he turned his back on us. And it's been that way since. I think he's a little embarrassed about his life, his lifestyle, you know his choices in life. You know, his best friend, and well, this buddy he's got who introduced him to the streets and got him selling drugs, now he's embarrassed…because *I* told him so. But he doesn't want to hear that so.

James described his future career plans and he expressed his interest in becoming a teacher:

In the future, I see myself teaching. 'Cause I can see myself influencing kids. I mean I think it's important that…when I was that age, twelve, thirteen, fourteen, growing up. I had people who supported me and helped me through life and I think everybody deserves that. You know, there are some kids out there who you might want to think they have support but they really don't. So the very few words you have to say to them in terms of encouraging them may be the first words that they hear and it may be the LAST! It just doesn't seem like people are trying to a…help each other out anymore. It just seems like well, "You do what you got to do, I mean, there's enough out there for you to figure it out for yourself." Not sit down and say, "Well, you're going to get in college next semester and I'm gonna to help you." You know what I'm sayin'? Exactly, yeah, not just school….BUT LIFE! I mean there's a lot of things you learn in school that you can apply to life. Just like there's a lot of things you learn in life that apply to school. So they go hand in hand.

James then shared about the influence of Charles' teaching on his decision to consider teaching as an option and his thoughts on the type of teacher he would like to become:

See he's wonderful! Charles offers a certain amount of play with them that they can feel comfortable and they seem like they can confide in him. But he also has this authoritative part of him, you know, he can give them one look and they all snap into just these little soldiers. I don't know if I have that. I can play with them…but when it's time to be the authoritarian…they're not going to listen to me because it's like, "No, you play with me all the time."

James discussed the stance that teachers need to have in the classroom to help motivate students to invest in academics:

So if you're asking me if a student came to me in the tenth grade and he's like, "Well, I want to be a scientist, but I don't think I have what it takes to be one, but that's what I want to be." No, you just got to practice. I mean we all are that. We all are scientists, we all are doctors, we all are lawyers, I mean it's just a matter of practicing. You know, practice makes perfect. Nobody's stupid, nobody's slow, nobody's remedial. It's just that you haven't had enough practice; you haven't applied yourself.

James envisioned how he would support students who were identified as academically behind as a tenth grade teacher:

Let's stick with tenth grade, that's a good time. They still have two years. I mean you'd be amazed what people can do in a matter of time. If they focus and really want it, um, I don't know, I'd probably assign them a mentor. Somebody they can work with and become comfortable with. 'Cause I'm thinking apparently they don't have that kind of practice at home or whatever they're doing to become the scientist. It's not really hard; it's just a matter of practice. But also I'll be realistic and give them other options. I'd say you want to be a scientist, but I'd give you other options in terms of career. I'm not trying to steer you away from it, but I want to keep your mind open. There are options; I mean…even personally, I think personality tests are pretty good, too. Well, I don't know, I just think that…well, I just think it's a good, well, they helped me. I don't think we really know enough about ourselves to say what we really like. So I'm thinking that personality tests are good because they just put on paper who you are and you have a chance to refute that. Say, "I don't really think that about me." The personality test could be right or wrong, but it gives you a chance to see what your options are. Your personality test may fit an astronomer, but you might not think that you could have been one. You're like, wow, I have that in me. You got it in you; you just don't know it's in you.

James offered a detailed account of how schools should be structured, which almost sounded like tracking. But he extended this idea beyond the typical notion of tracking by elaborating on how students would be exposed to advanced concepts at an early age:

But I think, I think there should be strata in school. Of course, you have the normal kids and then you have the remedial ones that you have to get up to par with everything else, but I think you should have at every pace along the way. You should have advanced kids, kids that by middle school can be doing calculus and can do physics. I mean there are kids out there that have the capacity; they just don't have the exposure. Let's say, for example, hypothetically speaking, I was that principal, I'd be very aggressive in having a program where kids could get, not AP for college credits, but where kids could get exposure to algebra, geometry, and trigonometry. Things that they're going to need in college. Starting earlier, much earlier. When they learn 2+2, they should learn square roots and exponential logarithms and stuff. So it wouldn't be so foreign when they get it there. I had thought about it. I guess I'm just so busy talking. Um, I was thinking about the advanced classes are important, but also I was thinking that it's important that they have internships as kids. Ten, twelve, fourteen years old, yeah, by all means, or part of the school week. I mean there's Saturday. I mean I think kids should go to school on Saturdays. Yeah, I mean they ain't doing nothing else.

James viewed his proposed structure as a means for offering supports based on a realistic understanding of students' strengths and abilities. He said, "I mean we have to be realistic but there are other options. I mean failure on top of failure is going to do something to him emotionally. So I mean he needs to know that there are going to be other options." Although James was not a father yet, he had visions about what he would like to pass on to his son:

If I had a son, I'd tell him don't stop. Don't give up; never give up. I'd probably go so far as to link him up with other people. Because I don't know, there's got to be somebody out there that knows. They got programs out there; you got mentors out there. Tutoring, you can get tutoring almost free. I'd probably be very active, even if I didn't finish school or have any degrees. I probably would be active and live vicariously through their academic life. I'd want to see great potential come from them.

He commented further on the role teachers should serve in supporting their students and their families:

As far as teachers are concerned, I mean it would help you understand my child, to understand me. I mean being uneducated is not the end of the world. So, I mean maybe some people might think it's something to be embarrassed about, but I mean it is a fact, if you have my child and my child is not educated, then you should know that I can't teach them and reinforce that at home. So maybe you can help me find other ways to reinforce that, like tutoring, after-school programs or maybe some place I can pay or take them and he'll get to learn. I don't know, I think they lose that connection with learning, with teaching the child. It becomes like a chair in your class or a bottle, it's not a child anymore. It becomes less and less about them, I guess. I think new teachers need common sense. Um, just the sense that not to carry your prejudices and your biases in the classroom with them. The sense that they don't understand the power of their position, 'cause I mean there's a lot of power in being a teacher. I mean, I can only imagine that it's probably the most rewarding job there is unless you just don't take it seriously, "Okay, well, everybody passed, get 'em out of here. Yeah, whatever." Maybe they should have some study-abroad programs in middle school, maybe kindergarten.

The stories Anderson family shared with each other validated their experiences as African American males while reinforcing the importance of education, despite any negative situations they may have encountered in school.

Important intergenerational themes, such as a sense of belonging to a community, the importance of education for future success, the threat of racism, the impact of negative images of African American males in the media, male role models, and the role of teachers in hindering or supporting their African American male students, were all raised in the Andersons' stories. These themes and others will resonate as well in the stories of the Wallace family, presented in the next chapter.

MEET THE WALLACES

My family wanted the best for me when I was a kid. Even when I didn't want it for myself, I had to make some mistakes before I could appreciate what they wanted me to do with my life.

-Family as described by Martin Wallace

I visited the Wallace family three times at their home and specifically the father twice at his place of work over a six-month period. I spent approximately two to four hours per visit. I conducted three interviews with Martin, the father, and his son, Tyreek, and two interviews with Malik. Each interview lasted approximately 45 to 60 minutes. As with the Anderson family, I noticed that over time the members of this family became more relaxed with my presence in their home. Sometimes a person would enter the interviewing space to ask the interviewee a question or make a comment about and then leave. Also, by the last round of interviews, there was again an expectation that I would stay for dinner or just remain to engage in conversation with them once the interviews were completed. The interviews I held with Martin at his office were in a large conference room, and when I expressed my concern about taking time from his work obligations, he assured me that he had cleared his schedule for us to talk. He told me he enjoyed our conversations.

DISCUSSION OF THE WALLACES

The Wallace family's stories speak to several important themes, such as safety, role models, access to resources, and positive and negative experiences with teachers. We also see how the theme of a sense of belonging to community permeates the stories

Table 4. Wallace Family Overview

Family	Relationship	Age	Education	Occupation
WALLACE:				
Martin	Father	48	1 year college	Project Manager
Tyreek	Son	11	5th grade	Student
Malik	Cousin	14	8th grade	Student

of all three males. For this father, his struggles in school led him to become involved in illegal activity and then to be incarcerated as a teenager. Once inside prison, his sense of not wanting to belong to the prison community led him, ironically, back to school. This sense of belonging to a community was now what he extended to the former inmate population he worked with.

His son was at this time seeking the physical and emotional safety of a new school, especially after experiencing disappointment and disillusionment at the hands of his current teacher. His cousin was also looking for that sense of community belonging on both sides of the classroom. His school's curriculum lacked positive images for him to hold on to for motivation. In addition, he and his teenage peers were being bombarded with negative images of themselves in the media. The stories of the African American males in the Wallace family demonstrate the importance of developing a self-motivating belief in education and access to resources to help individuals deal with adversity across different contexts and find the tools they need to transform their lives for the better. Given the nearly four decades that separate this father and son, what do each of them say about their schooling experiences across the decades? In their own words, hear the Wallace's stories.

Tyreek the Son: An 11-year-old Fifth Grader

Tyreek's story sheds light on the challenges urban African American boys face in school and in society. In his story, we see the influence of both supportive and non-supportive teachers and the influence of his peers on his schooling experiences. But more importantly, we find the influence of his father, Martin, on informing his experiences and the resiliency that is embedded in his young mind.

I conducted my interviews with Tyreek in the family's home; we usually sat at the dining room table to talk to each other. He had this to say about his overall feelings about school:

> School, it's been hard at times. At first I really didn't know everything, but I got used to it. The first couple of years was hard. It got easier as I went on. At first, I was like five or six; I didn't know my ABCs, even though most of the kids at that age knew. It was hard for me to learn it, but I figured out after a year. Then I got better at ABCs and 123s and I went to a new school after I got into second grade. I went to third, the kids knew multiplication by then and I didn't. I had struggled, so my mom wanted to keep me back cause I did not learn as good as the other kids.

He talked about having to make the decision to stay behind a grade, and its the academic benefits and social repercussions. At the time, he shared how his teacher wanted to let him move to the next grade, but his parents left the decision in Tyreek's hands. He decided to repeat the third grade. He shared how he had to deal with the challenge of being teased by some of his classmates for repeating the grade. He dealt with the situation by remaining focused on his work—and this strategy worked! His average that year went from the low 60s to the low 80s. He also pointed out how much he struggled with the area of writing.

For Tyreek, it was often a challenge to strike a balance between the high expectations of his teacher and the lack of engaging resources in his school; he commented:

> Well, at first when I thought about school, I thought it was prison. The only time you really speak in school is if you're answering a question or if you're in lunch. Yes, I could tell that my teacher had high expectations of us. He even made us read Shakespeare. That really wasn't for our level yet, but he made us read it. We had to finish it in like a certain amount of days; he gave us like a month or two. We read in class. We had to do a play and my whole family came.

He had this to say about his favorite teacher and the support she gave him:

> I liked her because she always helped me out when I was in third grade as a tutorer; she used to tutor me. And then I didn't know she was going to be my teacher, I was surprised and I was happy she was, cause I knew her and I knew she knew what kind of work I could do. The relationship I had with her before I was in her class really helped out.

Tyreek had much to say about his least favorite teacher and the lack of trust he had with him:

> My least favorite teacher is my teacher, Mr. James. He always put me...he didn't tell me messed-up things, but he told my parents messed-up things. Which they told me how he said I'm slow and retarded. About a student, why would you say that? He told my parents that I should get evaluated. Why would you tell my parents that? He never let us go outside like all the other teachers did. Even though we'd do the work, he never kept; he didn't try to keep his promises. He totally forgot about his promises, he said, "Y'all doing good work, I promise y'all, y'all will go outside"—it never came. We never got a chance to go outside and be with the other kids.

He went further to elaborate on his mistrust of this teacher's actions and how he believed he was spreading rumors about his academic issues with other teachers:

> It made me disappointed that a teacher would think about me like that, 'cause none of the teachers before thought about me like that. All the other teachers said I was a good kid and I did good work. Just that one teacher thought about me like that and that kind of disappointed me. I felt like I was giving him *nothing*. I still had to try to keep on going, though. I think I could have handled that, but the rumors my teacher spread to the adults about me being retarded would have made it difficult for me to stay there.

Tyreek went on to share his insights into how parents felt about this teacher's behavior and its potential impact on parental involvement:

A lot of the parents didn't like Mr. James; he'd have a meeting because he talked about whatever he wanted to talk about. He'd have a meeting with a printout schedule of what the meeting was supposed to be about, but he never followed that, every time he changed it up. The parents did not like that; sometimes parents didn't even show up. Then the parents don't feel like cooperating with you. Sometimes the parents are supporting their child and the teachers don't know and they're thinking that they're not.

Tyreek talked about his school experiences up until now and shared how he liked school but sometimes had teachers who did not like him. He said he knew this by the way they treated him and they did not seem to care whether he learned or not. This difference is illustrated by his earlier descriptions of the actions of his favorite and least favorite teachers. According to Tyreek, there are teachers who have low expectations of students of color, especially boys:

We thought fifth grade was easy, when we were in fourth grade, but apparently, no, it wasn't. I've had both Black and White teachers. My first teacher was over here at a school near my house. She was a nice teacher; she wasn't racist or anything. She'd teach us ABCs and 123s, it wasn't like the Black teachers were better—they were all about the same. It doesn't matter what color they are, it just matters if they have good teaching or not.

He shared how some of the other boys at school were performing and highlighted two of his friends who were at opposite ends of the spectrum. He talked about how his friend, Kalen, was not performing so well academically, while another of his friends, Lee, was pulling high grades because he is a better writer. Tyreek pointed out that writing was a valued subject for his teacher, Mr. James:

Some of the other boys in my class are not doing so good and some of them, they are. I have a friend, named Kalen, he's not doing as good, but I have others like my friend Lee, he does good, he gets nineties and hundreds. He does better writing work than me. We have to type and write a lot for Mr. James. He was very strict, you had to, well, he wanted a hundred percent. But you can't always do it, sometimes I pulled in a hundred percent and sometimes I did not. The greatest challenge was just to pass in his class.

Tyreek talked about the importance of school and his father's influence as a role model in his life.

My father helps me, well, he gets down on me. He rewards me if I do good. When he gets down on me, he gets strict, he says, "You can't do this, you can't do that unless you do better in school." Like I can't have no company over. Achievement to me means that I want to do something better with my life. I think that my father thinks achievement means me doing great things in life, like becoming a scientist. If I do, that will be a great achievement for me. Yeah, school is important! If you don't got no school, then it's no point in trying to make it in life. Because you're not going to make it in life without school. My father didn't become something that—he works for Connections, I mean he gets good money. But still, I could do better. And he didn't get there just laying around his whole life. He got there from going to school.

Tyreek talked about science being his favorite subject in school and how it was not a part of the regular school curriculum because his teacher focused on subjects he deemed more important:

I want to be a scientist, that's what I want to do. Because I always get good grades in science, I'm very good with science. Mr. James didn't know, he never asked and we didn't do much science in the class. If he asked, well, he might have put more science into class. Like I won a medal for my science project. The project is about how smoking can mess up your lungs. I first started out, the thing I wanted to do this for my mother, she smokes. I wanted to get a point over that smoking is bad. It took me two or three days to finish the diagram. Everybody else loved it in my school. Mr. James didn't really say anything to me. He didn't really care about science projects.

We discussed the impact that standardized testing had on the experiences of children in his class who do not perform well on such tests and the resulting negative treatment they received in school:

Tests tell you how good you are and where you need to upgrade yourself. They don't tell you everything, but they tell you where you need to improve, that's the most important thing and where you have got your stuff solid. When kids don't do well on tests, they give up. My teacher treated us differently because of how we did on the test. He separated the smart kids on this side and slow kids on this side. All the not smart ones were acting like fools. He paid more attention to the kids who were smart. The other kids were acting up because they wanted attention.

The issue of safety was important to Tyreek. He was excited about going to a new school in a safer neighborhood next year:

I'm going to a new school. So far I know that they have a good security, nothing really happens over there and that's what I'm happy about. In my old school when I used to walk home and stuff, I used to get jumped. Even the times I try to take the bus, before the bus came they caught me and they jumped me and took my cell phone. That doesn't happen in that school they have better security. Sometimes I have to worry about that in my neighborhood, but I don't have to worry about that all the time. I usually have my friends with me. I have to think about that, like if I have my iPod, I should keep that home, from then on I had to keep my stuff home. I had to have a cell phone but I didn't have a cell phone for like a month or two. So it was hard for me to communicate with my parents 'cause they didn't know I got home until I called them from the house phone. I don't have to worry about that around here a lot of times 'cause I know my friends got my back if anything goes wrong.

We had a conversation about African American boys and the challenges they face in school. Tyreek offered his opinion:

I don't think it's true that Black males are in so much trouble. It's kids around here that do good in school. I have friends that are smart, they're very smart, they go to my school. One of them is in a gifted school. It's kids around here that could do good in school. They all could do good in school, all Black kids, if they try and they keep on doing it.

Tyreek's previous comment demonstrates his belief that self-motivation is an important factor for African American boys to have. He discussed some of the dynamics he believed were at work with African American boys who struggled in school:

It's not that Black males don't want to, it's that they don't try to. Maybe 'cause they just feel like hanging around and smoking weed and stuff like that is the best thing for them to do instead of going to school. If I was in their shoes, I guess they think school is not meant for me, I don't feel like going to school. Maybe they struggled in school and they didn't ask nobody to help them. Sometimes people don't always help and if that don't work, just keep on asking, somebody will eventually answer you. Well, if that doesn't work I would get a tutor, and if that tutor doesn't work, I would ask for another tutor.

We talked about what achievement meant for some of the adults in his life. According to Tyreek, his fifth grade teacher, Mr. James, wanted him to do all of the work he assigned and that was achievement for him. He said, "He wants it done and if you did that you would be good." He added that his mother wanted him to eventually become the "chief officer in his own company." One adult's definition appeared to be more immediate and the other more focused on the future. Tyreek had this to say about the racial challenges he thought he might face as he got older and how he planned to handle this:

In the future, I might face White people trying to do better than me. And it's mostly White people out there that will be smart and I have to be smarter. I got to keep on at it. I got to be on top of them. I think there are some White people out there that don't want to see me do well because they would say something negative that will put you down and make them feel good. You shouldn't let that get to you and say, well, I'm a just keep on going, there's no stopping me.

Tyreek commented on what teachers needed to know about African American boys and what the boys needed to know about their teachers:

Kids need somebody to keep on telling them to do it, to motivate them, tell them don't slack. I think it's the parents and themselves and maybe even sometimes teachers who should tell them. If the did not have parents, then definitely the teachers should motivate them. Teachers need to know that, yes, sometimes Black boys don't feel like doing work, they get lazy at times. That happened to me sometimes, but I still got to do it. I'm not going to say all Whites; some Black teachers do it. They tell you negative things to get you down so you don't feel like doing it; you don't want to do it. It changes your mind even though you feel you want to. The negative.

He went on to offer his thoughts of the impact of racism on teachers' perceptions of their African American students:

White teachers feel that way because we was in slavery and ever since that they always thought of us as niggers—I'm not going to lie. They always thought of us as we didn't know better, we didn't know anything. That's not true. I mean look at Malcolm X, he was great, he did good. Look at Martin Luther King, he did good. Look at Barack Obama...he may not achieve what he really wants to, but he's still successful.

Tyreek shared his thoughts on the importance of teachers finding role models for African American students:

I've never had a teacher come in and talk about a Black man who's successful and alive, 'cause the first two are I mentioned are not. I think that if they did, that would encourage more Black males and even Black women, they have successful Black women out there. But they never say anything. That might be true that Black males don't have role models, but I think they can always find one, there's always a model out there. My father's a model for me.

Our conversation progressed to the public's perception that there is a dearth of role models for African American males. Tyreek commented on how role models existed within the community, but were often overlooked by teachers:

I don't think there's a lack of role models for Black boys, you just don't usually see them but they're out there. There was one guy, his name was Mr. Brooms. He looked for Black models throughout in the community and we didn't know. He found them. The person who works at Burger King across from our school, he was a Black role model—he was a manager there. He brought him into the classroom to talk to us, he told us how he achieved his goals and how he worked to achieve his goals to become a manager there. He started out as a peon and gradually he got to that, he owns that place. And we had another one and he was a fire worker. It doesn't matter what you are, even if you're an ice cream man, you can still be a Black role model. Sometimes it's true; fathers are not around, but even though fathers are not around, you could look for a Black role model.

Tyreek suggested that teachers themselves can be role models:

A teacher could be a Black [role] model, your best friend that's older than you can be a Black [role] model, your friend's father could be a Black [role] model; anybody can be a Black [role] model. You could even be a White [role] model—it don't matter! It's all about caring.

Tyreek talked about the influence of hip hop music, the lure of drug dealing, and the negative outcomes for Black boys who get involved in selling drugs at a young age:

I've been thinking like why kids go to jail so young, usually Black people, why? Maybe they didn't have nobody to support them in school, they could go to worst schools and still get good grades. I know kids around here that don't do good in school and they just hang around here late, till eleven or twelve o'clock at night. I be on my terrace around twelve o'clock, I be seeing kids walking around. I'll get killed by my parents. Maybe if I'm out the house or twenty-one. They learning stuff that they don't got to know; they drug dealers. Even though they got money, they don't live long. They might start at twelve and then live up to like twenty-four. The max is thirty. They choose the street 'cause that's the easiest way out. I mean you don't got to learn the streets, you can just watch and there you go, you know it like that. The school is a little bit harder and difficult. You got to learn to write, read, it just…even if you are going to go for the street, you got to learn how to do math. Because if you selling drugs, you gonna have to know how much you going to sell it for. You got to know how much you going to give the customer back. It don't matter what you do, you gotta deal with reading and math.

He went on to say how school was a better investment in the future than life on the streets:

But I wouldn't suggest you go on the street, because school's the easiest, the best way, 'cause you could do something and live a lot longer than a drug dealer and get paid a lot more.

We discussed the images that African American boys felt they have to project and how those images can conflict with what was expected of them in school:

I think a lot of Black boys feel like they need to be tough to survive, 'cause they think they can handle the streets. I mean the streets are dangerous. One day you be on the streets and then bam, you don't even know what happen, you be in the hospital somewhere, it don't matter. You could be a weakling and still be good in school. Fighting comes to the school, because kids think other kids are going to act like that. And then other kids get influenced by stuff like that and then it just spreads. It's like dog eat dogs. Kids be thinking I got to act tough 'cause everybody else is going to be tough and then everybody is just acting tough.

Tyreek talked about how certain images projected in hip hop music can have a negative influence on children and what teachers and parents should do to change this:

70

To get it to stop, well, you can eliminate the violence throughout the streets and I love hip-hop. But there's something about hip-hop that makes it do that. Hip hop with the drugs, the money, the pictures, and then the kids feel like they got to do all that have money, cars, bling-bling. People are buying into that.... Teachers need to know that some hip-hop is good; some are not appropriate. They can stop kids from listening to hip-hop inside the school and their parents can influence them to stop listening to it at home. I think that would help.

Next, we look at the schooling and life experiences of Tyreek's father and how the type of resiliency that Tyreek has inside himself was passed on.

Martin the Father: A 48-year-old Project Manager

Martin's story is one of overcoming setbacks and turning past negatives into future positives. Some of this he attributed to being lucky or being in the right place at the right time. He readily accepted his responsibility as a father and as a role model for his son. We can see parallels between his early schooling experiences and his son's current struggles with school. As Martin has turned his life around and now as well the lives of others through his choice of work, he was also serving as a father figure and role model to his son, Tyreek, and his teenage cousin, Malik.

Martin said the following about his earliest memories of school when he remembered having fun and being a good student:

Gosh, I remember all the way back to kindergarten. It was a lot of playing, a lot of finger-painting...a crush on the teacher, um. I remember walking seven or eight blocks to school with my mother. My mother, she would walk me to school everyday until about the third grade. It was equivalent to like two city blocks the long way 'cause I lived in the projects. Well, now it's a school for the gifted; when I went there it was just a regular old elementary school. But it was mixed. You had some Blacks, some Whites, some Spanish...the White kids came from another neighborhood. Ahh...up to the third grade, I actually was in the top classes. You know how you have the bottom first grade and then the top first grade. I was in the top classes until about the third grade.

Part of Martin's earliest memories dealt with a vision problem that affected his academic experience. In third grade, Martin had an undiagnosed vision problem that affected his ability to read and caused him to lose interest in reading. He remembered going from the top third of his third grade class to the bottom third because of his reading problem. His teacher at the time had students read out loud in class regularly, which was something he could not do. Martin offered the details of his reading issues and the problems he experienced with his vision:

I had a problem with reading out loud. I didn't have the confidence level. So everyday you were picked to go read to the class. That was that teacher's style. It probably worked for the other students, but it definitely didn't work for me.

I mean I actually didn't overcome that until probably tenth grade. And I never had that confidence to read out loud because I always felt I was reading too slow. Even though it would be accurate, but I just felt that it was too slow. I didn't find out till later on that what it was and what it boiled down to and even my son has the same thing. The muscle in my eye was weak. But back then, they sent you to the eye doctor and you read the chart, you know, they didn't have the real specialists then they have now. You know, they say "Does he need glasses?" and they'd say, "No, he has 20-20 vision." It wasn't to a point where they would really go into depth about what was happening.

Martin's vision problem went undiagnosed until he went to the College of Optometry, where it was discovered that the problem stemmed from the weakness of the muscle in his eye. He had to do exercises regularly to build up the muscle. He remembered his frustration at the time because until this diagnosis, he was told that his vision was perfect, but it technically was never "just a vision problem."

When he got to fifth grade, Martin was held back. He said, "Not because I didn't do the work, I did the work, but because my confidence level wasn't up to do the reading." Martin recently discovered that his son had the same issues with his eyes that he had when he was his age. He discussed the challenges he experienced in third grade and juxtaposed them with the challenges his son was also experiencing now:

I always push my son to do well in school. But, he's like how I was. He's always trying to be lazy, laid-back, I can see it. Well, my son got laid-back in the third grade and I used to tell my wife all the time, don't help him. He's got to struggle, he'll learn. She's like you're too hard on him, too hard on him, all the time. Even though for me, school wasn't hard, after third grade I had that gap, because I just wasn't really doing anything. I wasn't even really concentrating, I wasn't even trying to do the work, I was just...whatever. My school was traditional, but the way that the other people were teaching me in the program held my full attention.

For Martin, it was also in third grade that he began to disengage from school. He shared, "I'd be the last one to come in class, I was the first one out the door. I'd be the first one to throw something if the teacher was not looking. I was the class clown." He went on to discuss how the situation at school began to change for the better, thanks to an intervention by his fifth grade teacher:

Mr. Perry put me in this special group where half the day I would do regular school. Then the other half from 1 to 4:30, I would be in this special class for reading and they would help me, 'cause at one point I was at level 3 point something and I never made it past that. I was stuck there even in the fifth grade, because that was like two grades behind, so they didn't want to push me up.... I went to that reading program. I don't even remember what it was called, but it built up my confidence. And the way they taught me, it was a non-traditional way. Everything was through art and art was my thing.

This is what Martin had to say about the structure of the special program and why it worked for him:

> The timeframes were like high school, like you can be on a subject for a whole hour or you can be on a subject for like thirty minutes. So you get these short blasts of information, which I was able to focus on. Number one, it never hurt my eyes 'cause I never had to focus in on something for long periods of time. Two, I didn't have to read and I didn't have to focus long because it wasn't long. It was thirty or forty minutes, it was basically what a period in high school would have been. So I was able to retain the information. And then, too, they had rewards. I remember they had the cookie break; you'd have milk and cookies. They had lunch; they had the snack break just before we went home. You do a bit of work and you get rewarded and you do a little work and you get rewarded. If you messed up, you'd have to work during the cookie break. What happened was, really you got a chance to turn around and get it later. It worked for me.

As a result of this art-based reading program, Martin's academic performance began to improve but it also raised some suspicions, as he commented:

> I had an interest in art, so they made it interesting. The funny thing that happened was I went from the three point whatever to seven. In less than a year. Yeah, so they were like, how did he go from three point something to... something had to be wrong? They made me take it again because they were like how could he score this high; he had to cheat. I took it again; I had to, so I did. The way they did was they said they had made a mistake and then after I came out with the same exact mark, with the same exact answers and came out with pretty much the same exact grade.

He shared how his parents found out about what happened:

> Then the truth came out. 'Cause you know, back then parents...my parents knew a couple of people that worked in the school, 'cause you know back then most of the people that worked in the school was from the neighborhood—so you know, things leaked out. After that I just went to the next grade.

When he moved on to junior high school, Martin remembered being bused to a predominantly White school:

> And after that, when I got to junior high school I was still a little bored with school. Then I went to Monroe and there was more White kids there, basically I was bused. I rode the bus with White kids from my neighborhood. Then I was in class with a bunch of White kids and most of them wasn't. I have a mixed background so dealing with the White kids was like dealing with one of my cousins. Matter of fact, I only went there for two years.

By ninth grade, the pull of the streets began to take Martin's attention away from school, as his words revealed:

My last year, ninth grade, I was more getting into the street because school was kind of boring for me. During lunchtime I used to cut out and people's older brothers had jobs at the amusement park and we'd go do the ride thing… and the girls, you know. That's it, really harmless stuff compared to today. I mean there was no drinking, no drugs, no smoking, no cigarettes. It was kind of like harmless running around and having fun and riding the train, and stuff like that.

Martin went on to discuss the impact of busing on the community he grew up in and how the large class sizes affected his interest in school:

I think certain classes I just never took an interest in. Back then Spanish wasn't mandatory. The teacher just really wasn't a good teacher, I mean he taught me some Spanish that I still know today but um, I think the classes were a little bit too large back then. Because we used to have thirty-five to thirty-eight people to a class back then. We're talking about the Eighties, I mean the classes were pretty packed. And my neighborhood didn't have a junior high school because my neighborhood's junior high was for the gifted. So we didn't have a junior high school, so they'd bring us to the next neighborhood. We had three junior high schools, but you're talking about a huge neighborhood. So when you're talking about the whole neighborhood, kids were getting bused to another neighborhood.

Safety became a major issue once Martin started to cut classes and visit friends at other schools. He talked about how he navigated the existing racial tensions in high school because of his connection to some of his White friends in junior high. Martin shared that while busing to desegregated schools, it did not change the attitudes of the different groups of students who were encountering each other for the first time in school. According to him, racial tensions flared regularly:

Outside the school, you might not be that safe 'cause there was a lot of racial tension…. But for me, a lot of times because I went to the junior high school that I went to, I already knew those White guys, I had already knew them three years before I even got there. And when I got there, even the older ones they knew me because they knew me 'cause I used to go to their houses 'cause their younger brothers were my friends and now here's the older brothers. So I never had a lot of problems with them because I got along with people…. Now for some of my friends, now that's a different story! That's a whole 'nother different story—we used to get the heads up. They'd say, "Yo M, go out through the back 'cause we getting them niggers today." And they was serious, they was dead serious.

Martin talked about how these racial tensions were acted upon outside of school and not in the classroom. According to Martin, the rules of the classroom were set by the adults, and there was an unspoken code between the students not to air their racial problems in class to avoid adult intervention. For Martin, being on the football team came with its own unspoken "academic benefits":

> That was a big thing back then, the football team. And then plus the coach used to always tell us, "Make sure you go to class and you'll pass." We always made sure we showed up. Well, some classes I wouldn't show up because I knew the work. I had a couple of teachers that knew I knew the work because it was a thing of being responsible because how can I see them second period, skip their class fourth period, and then I'm walking right past them at seventh period. I was one of the students who could handle the work whether I went to class or not.

According to Martin, his father was serious about his son doing well in school and in his life. At the time, Martin did not share the same self-motivation and investment in the future and relied on the social capital he felt he had. But he later discovered, with his father's passing, that was not the case:

> Being mediocre, I didn't have to think I could just show up. I used to sit there and look at the kids who were at the top of the class and say, "Tss, that's crazy." So every day I had money and new clothes. A lot of times those kids just didn't have means, because they used to come over to my house and I used to go to their house and I'd see a big difference. I was like, wow, but I never associated that with that's why they were busting their butt because they were trying to move up a notch. I felt I was already up that notch they trying to move up to. So, why am I gonna work any harder at this when I didn't have to? Well, my father already had his own business and my friends would say, "Oh, all you need to do is finish high school and boom, you got a job!" It didn't turn out that way, my father kept his business until he died and then my mother sold it.

Martin shared the details of becoming less involved in school and becoming a teenager involved with illegal car trafficking, which eventually led to two years in prison:

> So, but on my last year, school was getting a little too boring and I was making a little bit too much money hanging out. Back then I was running with these guys who, they would steal cars and they would take 'em and sell 'em. Then I met some guys who were friends of my cousins on the other side of my family, on the Italian side of my family. They said, if I bring these cars to these people I could make some nice money. Now you know, for a kid sixteen, fifteen years old, five hundred dollars, that's a lot of money in the Eighties. That was a lot of money, I averaged two, three cars a week.... What happened was, I went somewhere to go get a car, and the police got involved. And I got away, I just drove slow, but the guy who I got to come with me, he got caught. Of course, he told everything. But he was older than me, he got caught.

In an attempt to avoid prosecution, Martin asked to be sent away for a while and his parents obliged by sending him to stay with family in the South, as he commented:

I was in South Carolina, close to the borderline of North and South Carolina. Then I came back and when I came back I got a little job for a company down in the Wall Street area. I was staying with one of my cousins that was a little older. And the cops came in the building and I didn't have any ID, so they stop me and that's when my secret indictment came up. That's when you get indicted on the word of another person who testifies to the grand jury. Which was the guy who got caught. They sentenced me to eighteen months; actually it was two years.

While in prison Martin decided to take advantage of the work release program and go back to school. For Martin, being in prison was about constantly doing the same things over and over again, and being locked up with guys who were fighting for their lives. Martin found that prison was a microcosm of society, especially with regard to dynamics around race, ethnicity, and national origin. He also discovered there were even tensions around degree of skin color. School became a refuge for him while he served his sentence:

I learned very quickly, even though I was only on Rikers Island for forty-five days, I learned a lot just from watching. What really hit me first was the separation of color, Black, White, Spanish. I came from a neighborhood and schools where that was a mixture. So that was a whole new thing to me. That was one of the first things, before if you were light-skinned Black I learned a whole other kind of prejudices that I never paid attention to. The light-skinned versus dark-skinned, the Caribbean versus American. I was listening to a lot of the older guys, the adults.

Martin connected with some of the much older guys, but realized that he did not want to share their fate. He received a wake-up call when working as an aide for a drug counselor. This experience helped him see the value of education and choosing a career that would impact people's lives:

I got a job as an aide to the drug counselor. That also helped me want to learn how to work with people because it was like a wake-up call....reality! 'Cause you could have a job that has no impact on other people or you could have a job that has impact on other people. I learned that in there. 'Cause I was like, why are there so many people working in the kitchen and the offices there's only like one inmate. In every office there's only one person...you go to the cafeteria and there's like droves. So many, it's like working in a factory, and that's the one that has no impact. That's where I learned there is a difference in classes. That was one of my first things I learned, that people judge you by how much you earn, what your education level is.... I knew that work was something that you had to do.

Martin reflected on his past life and lamented over some of the poor choices he felt he had made in his youth. He shared what motivated him to do the reform work he currently did:

So you know a lot of lessons were learned and you know, I got a lot of breaks. Which kinda made me sharper, I guess. At the end, I look at all those life experiences and I thought, you know what? It didn't have to go that way. A lot of things could have went another way which could have end up me being a whole 'nother type of person. That's why I been working in the system for a long time, working in jails. If you go to my desk right now, you'll see a whole bunch of mail from inmates from all over. They're asking about jobs, training, housing, all those issues I talk about. I might go to Sing-Sing again. So I figure even though I was in trouble when I was young, I got lucky enough to get that certificate on the day of sentencing. If I didn't have it, my whole life would have been different.

Martin discussed the dynamics at work at the school in the South and the educational experiences he shared with other males in his family around how they were disciplined in school:

It wasn't even like I knew that the street thing was the thing to do. That was like the commercial in my life; the main thing was that I knew I had to work. And I knew that when my father came to the Northeast at fifteen, he dropped out of school in the seventh grade down South. Well, I was lucky enough to go to the school for a bit down there—the school my father went to. There it's not like here. The school was on Lake Paul Wallace in Venice Ville on the coast. The same guy who was the principal when my father was there was the same principal when I got there. We used to call him Ole' Fess....old professor. And he lived on the grounds, like they did when my father was there; he lived on the property and I guess he watched the property at night. I guess like real old times. He was Black and when I got there, the differences in that school was they used to tell you that detention or a beating. And he had this fiberglass, thick square chunk. It wasn't no paddle. And that's what he would hit you with, like "WACK!" but it wouldn't break. I've seen him hit some good ones. Back then, I think it was '79 or '80, it was what your grandparents went through, and your parents went through it 'cause they came from that school, so you went through. So remember it was a town thing, the whole culture was different.

Martin compared the discipline of his day and how he responded to it versus how children of today respond to discipline:

Here, you hit a kid and it's like "Yo, we ain't havin' it." Down there it happened to me I lived through it, you got to go through it. When I went home and I complained to my grandfather, he said, "Well, you shouldn't have did what you did," and that was the end of the conversation. I got on the phone with my father, he told me the same thing, "You shouldn't have did what you did and that's what you get." That's the way they do it down there.

Martin shared what he knew about what his father's life was like in the South and why he moved North:

Well, what happened with my father was he came home one day and he had a dog and the dog's name was Sport. The dog had did something and my grandfather was one those real ornery types, like just can't stand everybody type people and he killed his dog. And my father got mad and my father had a car and he was fed up. He had a little job up the block at this little store, he took his money, he took his car, and he drove up to here to go stay with my great uncle, which was my grandfather's brother because he just had enough of my grandfather, his father…. And he came up here and he washed dishes and eventually he got a job at this place that sold shrimp to the Chinese restaurants. And after he did that for a while, he never went back to school. He got his own business, he had a yellow cab and that's when he started working for himself. Back then yellow cabs drew over forty thousand dollars and that's what he did. But school was a big thing with him, even though he didn't finish he was always pushing me and "Yo, you got to do this, you got to do that." And I push my son the same way.

Martin expressed his concern over his son Tyreek's investment in school and the lessons he has learned from his own schooling experiences. Martin saw that his son was not very motivated to push himself to do better with his schoolwork:

What I can see in my son that all he wants to do is enough to get by and I recognize that and it drives me crazy. 'Cause I know if I would have sat there and said, maybe if I would have pushed myself I'd have been too busy to get into all the other stuff. 'Cause when you are just doing it and you're just getting by and you're not having to worry or study. I can remember the only times I ever studied was when I was in college. Even in the first semester, I had gotten such good grades and it wasn't because all the time I had studied or I wanted to. I studied because I had nothing else to do, either that or draw.

Martin talked about his son's struggles with being left back and how he motivated him to do his work at home:

Now he's actually doing the homework and the teacher is actually seeing a big difference. And I come home, sometimes I have to do work on things and I come home, and I'll ask, "Did you do your homework?" Now I learned what I have to do is say, "Let me see it." Now I see that he's actually trying to be independent, but that wasn't happening at the beginning of the year. I know he has that in him because that's how I used to do. Right now he's saying, I know I have to do this because I don't want to get left back. It's bad enough my son already started the year behind from the jump.

Martin offered his opinion on why Black boys were not performing well in school and he had a great deal to say about the current state of affairs:

Public school is only going to give you history and people that most African American and Latino kids cannot relate to. You ask a kid today well who is

Malcolm X, he's probably not going to really know. Same thing with Martin Luther King, it doesn't make a difference that it was only thirty, thirty-five years ago. It doesn't matter, it has no significance to it anymore for them. This whole generation of kids, you ask them who is Jay Z, because that's somebody that they know that's alive and a role model there for them. It may not be the role model that most parents want. And that's really because my generation came up short. Because the generation before that wanted to make change, the way my generation wanted to make changes and not do the same thing that our parents did.

We also discussed the role of community in raising African American males and, according to Martin, times have changed for the worse:

And probably but in reality we needed to keep those same tradition forms. Like for example, my son's friends see me and they call me by my first name. If I did that when I was a kid, I'd have got knocked upside my head. But it would have been Mr. So-and-so or Mrs. So-and-so, maybe not even a first name. I mean I see a kid in the street and they cursing like a sailor, well, that was unheard of. You don't never let an adult hear you. Now whether or not you're cursing around your peers, you could be like a sailor around them, but as soon as you see Miss Marley, you better, you better straighten up. Act right. They don't even try to act right. They just like it's acceptable for them to not have respect.

Martin went further to discuss what he believed was the "missing piece" in today's schools:

So I feel like there's a big piece missing.... I think what happens is most African American kids need to have a work ethic slash school type thing going on.... They need that hands-on experience, certain things like home economics; I remember having that when I was in high school. The point is if you are missing a lot of these little things, then how are you going to jump to the big things? There's no base, there's no base, so if you don't make sure your kids know how to do these little things, how are you going to expect your kids to comprehend and understand the bigger pictures? You can't because they have no foundation, there's no foundation. I don't think any schools do that right, it doesn't matter if they're Black, White, Spanish or what; it doesn't make a difference. I mean between the budget cuts and both parents having to work, the community.

Martin specifically addressed what African American males need to understand about the image they project and how it limits their access in society. He cited the media and the music industry for projecting negative images to African American males that they buy into all too often today:

The image that you project gives you greater access to greater opportunities. How to deal with knowing how to conduct yourself in different situations, that's something that Black boys are going to have to learn from everywhere. But today, if you sat there and talked to a young person because of the movies and the music videos and all that, a drug dealer is viewed much differently because the media, the music industry is portraying drugs, rap music and those girls. You got something on TV that's glorifying everything that's negative. The kids don't stand a chance. You get the mixed messages; you got what corporate America says and what school says. You got two different pictures. The only reason that I look at it differently is because of the path that I took and I got a couple of breaks, so it gave me the opportunity to start looking at things differently.

For Martin, today's community has changed and this also takes a toll on supports for African American boys:

The community is different now. When I was growing up, I knew everybody in my community, and if I didn't know them, they knew me. And if they didn't know me by name, they definitely knew whose kid I was. That was a definite. Now I see little kids, you don't know who they are or who they belong to.

Martin shared his hopes for his son Tyreek's future and he talked about the advantages Whites have over people of color in the job market. He shared with me what he told his son to prepare him for the harsh realities of inequity within society. He offered an example of how he tried to provide real-life examples for his son to digest about the consequences of making bad decisions in life:

I remember I'd bring my son down to my job in the corrections office and he'd see the guys in the green jumpers and he'd ask, "Well, what did they do?" And I'd say some of them made some bad decisions and it caught up with them. So now they are on lock-down. Now this is what they got to do. Go to place like this and wait around and hope that they get a job or they sometimes got to work for free. He said, "What do you mean, like a slave?" I said yeah, pretty much. People tell them what to do all day and they can't really say no. Even the companies they work for exploit them because they know they need to keep a job to stay off the street. They can't afford to lose that gig 'cause they trying to get freedom. Hey, they should make an American Express commercial. "Freedom, it's priceless!" And then close the door of a cell—clank!

When we talked about how he supported his son academically, Martin shared a recent story about finding a book that he felt would interest his son:

Like right now, I've got him reading this book; I have to be creative with him. He's not the type of person that's going to want to read a book on his own. The book is *The Notorious C-O-P*. It's about the first hip-hop police. So first when I told him about the book, he said, "Nah, I don't want to read no cop book."

He further piqued Tyreek's interest by letting him listen to the music of the artists in the book he was reading:

When he read the second chapter about people like Rapper's Delight, people like Kane and all these other old-time rappers, Grand Master Flash and all that, and I let him hear the music, he got interested because he could make some type of connection. Where it was like it caught his interest just enough to keep him that I don't have to twist his arm to read it.

We had a conversation about his hopes for the new school that his son would be going to next year and how he hoped the changes in the school structure would help him do better in school:

I don't know right now, my son ain't feeling his school. He was really struggling, struggling, struggling with the basics. So if you're struggling with the basics, it's hard to kind of get through the rest. So we're trying to fix it. He's going to a new school next year out in Manta Beach area. It's a public school; my sister has a house over there. This school is much bigger. They have three fifth grade classes, three sixth grade classes, three seventh grade classes, and three eighth grade classes. The bigger school part is the disadvantage, but the speed of the class is the advantage because they'll be able to match it. So maybe he won't have to struggle so hard. Schools with one class per grade, there's no flexibility. The pace is set and that's that.

Martin expressed his concern over finding a good alignment between a teacher's area of interest and the student's area of interest:

His other teachers at the school he's been at for the past three years were pretty good. It's hard to gauge each teacher, because like Tyreek has good math skills, maybe that was the previous teacher's strong point with kids. Maybe English wasn't it. So that really doesn't have anything to do with the student that has something to do with the teacher. You're not going to be able to get great English students out of a great math teacher. If math is their forte, then that's what it is. A lot of the student's success depends on the student's area of interest. People go for whatever's the easiest for them. If math is a natural thing, where you can do with ease, then you're going to gravitate to a job that you could do easily. No matter how hard the job may be to somebody else.

In one of our last conversations, Martin commented on the role of the extended family in the African American community and he commented by referencing his time in the South as a teenager:

I didn't go down there a lot and for me to have to go down there to go to school, I mean it was pretty much like my father just threw me down there. I had gotten in trouble but it wasn't big, but I was having a lot of fights and stuff. Kids are still getting sent to their grandparents if there's a problem. See but what happens now is that they're not sending them down South because the grandparents are still living here in the city. The kids aren't going anywhere, which is one of the pieces of that quick fix that was good. 'Cause you need to take them and then put them in a different element. But, if you're just taking them from one household and putting them in another household, that may not be enough. So you don't have that total independence, so you have grandparents saying, "Well it's my way or nothing," and kids can say, "Well, I'm going back to my mother's house." You ain't going to do that from five hundred miles away.

Martin talked about the benefits of being with extended family in the South and hearing the stories that were passed down from generation to generation:

The benefits of my going down there is that now as an adult I'm closer to them. I have a great-uncle who's ninety that I try to go visit every summer. My son's been down there to visit, it's like he knows who they are but he doesn't know the importance. 'Cause when kids his age go down there, it's about running in the back, let me see what snakes I can find. It's not about like he let me sit down and listen to some of these stories. I don't know when he'll be ready, but me, when I was living down there I got to hear them regardless. I was stuck there, so that's why I'm going to let him stay there for two weeks. It's going to be interesting for him, he's going to see how small, small towns are and it will make him understand that your neighborhood is the same way. How people know you, but you're like I ain't never seen you before. Down there it's like that, as soon as they see the new face they know exactly who you are. That's right. That teaches you that you're not invisible, so that whatever you do there's always people watching you. In a good way in that sense.

Martin gave his son advice and support based on his past experiences and his understanding of how society operates on multiple levels. He also played an important role in the life of his nephew, Malik. Now we will hear about Malik's schooling experiences.

Malik the Cousin: A 14-year-old Eighth Grader

Malik's story offered insights into the understandings of teenage African American boys that are absorbed from their schooling experiences in some urban schools. Teachers' perceptions played an important role in how students supported their own learning and how they supported the work of their teachers. Malik's story acts like a bridge between the stories of his uncle and his younger cousin. He was old enough to have a strong sense of the dynamics at work in the school, but he also held on to a youthful resiliency that allowed him to dream of a positive future for himself, despite the many negative situations he had to deal with in school. As Malik shared his earliest memories of school, he talked about a negative experience he had with his third grade teacher:

I remember my third grade teacher just ignored me. I was quiet at first, and then the only way I got attention from her was when I fooled around. So I started fooling around a whole lot. She would be telling my mother I was a behavior problem. My mother would come in and sit in back of the classroom and I was fine. But that was when the teacher would pay good attention to me when my mother was there. She was putting on a show for my mother. When my mom wasn't there, it was back to business as usual.

Malik talked about how this teacher's perceptions informed the experiences of some of his classmates as well:

I got a reputation of being a behavior problem. She didn't know what to do with me 'cause I was smart and would do her work. I just didn't like that teacher and she didn't like me. Come to think of it, a lot of my friends' mothers would be doing the same thing. And she be putting on the same show. She was racist and on top of that she couldn't teach. I had other teachers like that, too.

He shared his feelings about what he thought of school at the present time and the lack of African American history in the curriculum at his school:

School is boring, boring, boring! We learn about all the great things that White people have done, but we hardly ever learn about what Black people have done for society. Only time we learn about Black people is during Black History Month. I know enough about Martin Luther King and Harriet Tubman already—I could write my own book about them. But what about all the other Black people that have contributed to society, to the world? We get cheated out of our history, it's like we don't have a history. Thank God we have computers now, I can look up stuff on my own.

Malik offered his opinion of his teachers and their lack of investment in their African American students:

I feel like my teachers don't know me, and they don't really care. They don't encourage me, whether I do good or bad, it's like they don't care anyway. Even some of the Black teachers don't care. Everybody just cares about the tests and that's why I say school is so boring. They act like Black kids don't want to be nothing, like we don't have dreams or nothing.

He shared his insights into why African American boys may not be doing well in school and his impressions of his school. He also shared his goals for the future:

A whole lot of my friends are smart; some of them are smarter than the teachers! But they Black boys and when you a Black boy, nobody expects you to be smart; nobody wants you to be smart. The girls get treated a whole lot better than the boys. We get treated like we gangsters and thugs, like we two seconds away from pulling a trigger. We had metal detectors in my old school; it was like training for prison. I didn't feel safe; some of those security guards were like the Terminator. Me, I just felt late because it takes forever to get into the school because the guards go through your stuff like you got a bomb or something. We had got a new principal but it was more of the same. Get to class, don't talk, hurry up and get to class! Some of the teachers didn't mark us late, but a whole lot of them did!

One teacher in Malik's school seemed to be supportive of the students and they reciprocated that support in their own way:

> I got one teacher now, Mr. Harris, he's cool. He tells us like it is and gets us to work. We look out for him just as much as he looks out for us. You know, like when the principal or somebody comes to his class, we sit up and quiet down, 'cause that's what they want to see. But he lets us be as long as we get our work done. He says discipline is about getting your work done by any means necessary. He said we don't have to be little machines to be successful, just be smart to know that somebody is always watching us. And he's right, we always being watched.

Malik commented on the lack of encouragement from the teachers at his school and how most of the students had unrealistic views of the future:

> The rest of the teachers don't talk to us about the future, just the right now and the right now is what they want us to do, not what we want to do. Everybody at my school wants to be a rapper or a basketball star—it's a trip, 'cause people being saying that just because that's what everybody says. Some people don't even, can't play ball or rap. It's crazy.

He had this to say about the encouragement he received from his uncle, Martin:

> My Uncle Martin be telling me that I'm smart and I can do other things that will give me more satisfaction with my life. Like my cousin Tyreek and I are going to do business together, we're going to design computer games. That's where the money is.

I asked Malik about his father and the African American males who served as role models for him:

> I don't know my father, he's around but he's a stranger to me. He used to come around when I was a kid. But I hardly see him now. Martin is more like a father for me. He's cool and he's smart. He my role model, he went through stuff when he was younger, but he has a good life now and he takes care of his family.

He talked about some of the negative behavior of some of his peers and where he thought they would end up:

> I know dudes that are making stupid choices, like drugs and stealing stuff. You know exactly where they gonna end up. Oz, and it ain't no HBO show. I don't want that for me and it's hard 'cause dudes be bragging about stuff and showing off and sometimes you want stuff too. But you got to be smart and want to live better than that. Going to jail is like going to the grave. Most dudes get lost there, more lost than when they was out here.

Malik commented on the images of African American males in the media and the disconnect between the lives of boys and their teachers' awareness of the challenges they faced:

> Martin, my uncle, tells us all the time that he was lucky. But it's not a chance Tyreek and me can afford to take. My mom is always working to take care of me and she says it'll break her heart if I get in trouble. And if I do, she said she ain't coming to see her baby behind no bars for nobody! I just try to mind my business and stay out of other people's business. I'm not trying to be in the wrong spot at the wrong time if I can help it. Besides, there's nothing on these streets but trouble. On the streets nobody's got your back, you're on your own, it's mad crazy. Nah, me, I want people to be reading about me and not with my head ducking cameras in no newspaper. That's like the only time you see a Black man in the news is with his hands behind his back, cuffed up.

In our last interview, Malik addressed the disconnect between his teachers and their students:

> The teachers don't know what we go through everyday just getting back and forth from school and they ain't trying to hear it neither. My teachers wouldn't be caught dead around here, maybe that's the only way they'd come around here. It's like two different worlds, two different universes. They act like they in a galaxy far far away, and us, we stuck on the dark side of the moon. I know I'm smart and I'm going to make it for me and my family.

Through the intergenerational stories of the Anderson and Wallace families, several recurring themes have been identified. These themes are also present in the schooling experiences of the Freeman family. In Chapter 7, we next learn about the males in the Freeman family and their experiences with school.

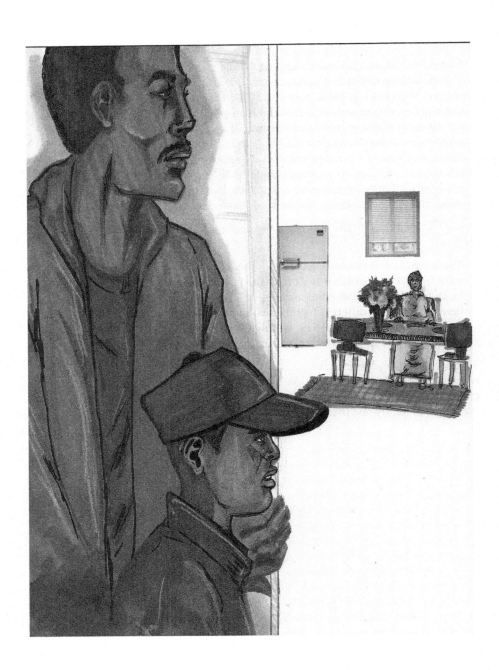

CHAPTER VII

MEET THE FREEMANS

Growing up and knowing that I am loved by my family has helped me make it through some tough times in my life.

-Family as described by Joshua Freeman

I visited the Freeman family five times at their home over a six-month period. I spent approximately three to four hours per visit. I conducted three interviews with Joshua and Tyrone, and two interviews with Jacob and Larry. Each interview lasted from approximately 45 to 60 minutes. As with the other two families I interviewed, I noticed that over time the family members became more relaxed with my presence in their home. They too would often ask each other questions and engage in side conversations during the interviews. By the completion of my last interviews, I received an invitation to attend a large family dinner before Grandpa Jacob returned to his home in the South. It was a powerful learning experience to see and listen to all the generations of African American males talking about the value and purpose of education at one time. It was a layered story come to life.

DISCUSSION OF THE FREEMANS

The stories of the Freeman family offer an intergenerational portrait of the issues and challenges that African American males continue to grapple with in school and society. For all of the members of this family, there was an underlying belief that education is important: from the youngest male, Tyrone, whose schooling

Table 5. Freeman Family Overview

Family	Relationship	Age	Education	Occupation
FREEMAN:				
Joshua	Father	23	HS graduate	Store Clerk
Tyrone	Son	10	4th grade	Student
Jacob	Great Grandfather	73	HS graduate	Retired
Larry	Cousin	22	College Graduate	Office Assistant

experiences had not yet shown him just how important it can be for him; to Larry and Joshua, whose experiences—both positive and negative—allowed them to embrace the value of education and make plans for the younger generations to follow, and finally to Jacob, the oldest male, whose experiences of schooling in the segregated South to life in the desegregated North allowed him to see mistakes made concerning their children's education and how change for African American males will only come about when their education is made a top priority by everyone involved in their lives. The span of age difference between the Freemans nearly doubled that of the Andersons and the Wallaces: 63 years, six decades, separate the elder, Jacob, from his great-grandson, Tyrone. What did they say about their schooling experiences across the decades? In their own words, hear the Freeman's stories.

Tyrone the Son: A 10-year-old Fourth Grader

Tyrone's story raised issues that many low-income urban African American boys face in schools. It is commonly known that the some of the worst teachers can be found in the most under-resourced urban schools. Issues of mistrust and threat of violence ran through Tyrone's story like a speeding train. His story is one of resiliency against overwhelming odds that education for him and boys like him was not helping them envision a brighter future.

When he shared his schooling experiences with me, Tyrone began by talking about a problem he had been encountering with one of his classmates:

> There's a boy in my school who's twelve and in the fourth grade, he's always teasing me saying I'm dumb. But he's dumb, I'm in the right grade and I'm about to go to fifth grade. So he's dumb. And one of my aunts is thirteen and she's in the eighth grade. So he's supposed to be in at least the seventh or the eighth. He trying to call everybody dumb and he might be the oldest and the tallest in my class. Yo, he mad dumb, 'cause he got to use a calculator to do his times tables and stuff.

Tyrone then transitioned into talking about the problematic behavior of the administrators and teachers at his current and former schools:

> In my school there's a lot of problems, the teachers are mean, the principals lie and the teachers lie. They be bothering the kids and they lie to the parents and say, "Your kids be acting up" and stuff. The other thing they say is that this is a great school for children and stuff. So they going try to lie and stuff so they can just be mean to the kids. My teacher pushed me one time 'cause I didn't want to take off my coat. I need a tape recorder to record some of the teachers who be cursing. I had a teacher at my old school say when there's witnesses around she won't hit me, when they're not she will—that's why I changed schools. I think if parents could hear what teachers say to kids sometimes, they wouldn't be friends with them.

He shared the best thing he liked about his school: "My school goes up to junior high school. It's just that I'm on an elementary level. It's a third through eighth grade. The best thing I like about school is my friends." Here he described his interest in science and talked about wood shop, which happened to be his favorite class:

> I've done a lot of science experiments. I made up my plant and my plant is growing real big and I get to do would shop. I'm good at wood shop, I made a rectangle and it says my name. And I made that for my sister and I made a puzzle out of wood. I designed it myself and I cut the wood out, they let the kids do that. Wood shop is my favorite class.

This is what Tyrone had to say about music, his least favorite class, and why this was the case for him:

> The class I don't like the most is music class, because it's supposed to be music and we be watching movies. I understand we be watching the kid movies, but if this is music class, then why can't we do music? We have instruments and we used to do instruments, but I don't know why we not doing them no more. When this is music class, then why we don't deal with music?

He also shared what he was doing in reading and math at school:

> There are ten other kids in the class with me; there are three girls and seven boys. I read good, and I did at least six or seven book reports. I don't read Dr. Seuss books now, but if I had to choose, that would be my favorite one: *The Cat in the Hat*. I read the whole book and I saw the whole movie. I like math, my favorite thing to do is pluses and takeaways, and the times table. I don't like dividing 'cause I mess up on dividing.

Tyrone talked about his friends at school as protectors against the threat of violence:

> My friends have my back, especially if I was going to get jumped. But my friend Davone, 'cause like he'll come out of his classroom and stuff to like just help me. Like if an older kid try to stomp on me and stuff, like my friend, Davone, he'll be behind me.

For Tyrone, playing basketball is a catalyst to getting a better education. He also shared his notions of what he would do in the future if basketball was not an option:

> I think I'm supposed to do good in school. I want to get a good education and I want to play basketball. You don't need that much education to play basketball, but I need a scholarship. If I couldn't do basketball, I want to do football. If I couldn't do football, well, I'll just go get a regular job and do paperwork or something. I would need an education and they would need to see my papers, my grades, averages and things, my grades need to be right.

In describing his relationship with his school counselor, Tyrone revealed why a breech in promised confidentiality led to his lack of trust:

My counselor talks to me about stuff like that. She tells me whatever I tell her stays in her office. But that's not true because she lies to me, she tells everybody else. She tells the principals and the teachers everything. I don't trust her. I don't talk to her no more.

As a result of no longer trusting his counselor for support, Tyrone now relied on himself for emotional support in school and on his grandmother outside of school:

When I'm at school, my counselor is myself. When I'm outside of school, then my counselor is my grandmother. I have a counselor for speech and anger management class. I have a lot of anger to everybody in the world. I don't even know how to say why I have it.

In Tyrone's eyes, his biological father supported his siblings more than him. He commented on how his stepfather, Joshua was more of a supportive father figure in his life now:

My father, he don't pay any attention to me and my older brother and I have two different fathers. But he be calling my father Daddy and my father spends more time with him than with me. And I feel like I don't have no father because he don't pay attention to me, he don't care about me. Joshua is like my father now. He looks out for me now. Me and my brother have a really good relationship. It's just that we always fight. I see my real father once every couple of months. Me and my father used to run and play around when I was like four years old.

I asked Tyrone to tell me about his relationship with Joshua, his stepfather, and he shared how he motivated him to want to do well in school:

Joshua talks to me about school sometimes, he'll be like, "Are you doing good in school?" And I got to do good in school and get a good education. That makes me think that I have to be good in school to play basketball. I have to be good to show all my family that I can be somebody in life. I get along with my mom all right. She talks to me about school sometimes. She say the same things that Joshua be saying. My real father doesn't say nothing to me about school because I don't talk to him. He's working, he lives somewhere else. Joshua knew me since I was like one year old, 'cause he was friends with my uncle before he got with my mother and he still is.

Tyrone talked about his relationship with his 26-year-old uncle and the things he enjoyed doing with him:

My uncle lives in the next building away from my grandmother. He's what, twenty-six, and he plays games with me 'cause he still have a kid inside of him. He acts like an adult because he is one, but sometimes he be like playing games. We be having water fights in the summer and he be playing with us. He be on me and my brother's team and it be like all the boys against the girls. We have buckets and water guns.

Tyrone went on to comment about male role models and how he viewed himself as his own. He said, "I act like my dad because I be wearing a lot of matching clothes. I think of myself as a role model. I just want to be myself." He commented on his teachers as role models and expressed his thoughts on why teaching as a career did not appeal to him:

> My teachers don't talk to me about my future. I don't want to be a teacher because I start thinking that I'll end up treating my students the way that my teachers treated me and I don't want to do that. Teaching is a bad thing for me because I haven't been around a good teacher.

He elaborated further by recounting an early memory of when he had good teachers in pre-kindergarten and what that experience was like:

> My pre-K teachers were good teachers, 'cause we had breakfast at school and they made it. We got to decide what we wanted. All those teachers was nice. We got to be with them when they went on the bus to get food and we did homework and stuff. And we got to trace the ABCs on a piece of paper.

Tyrone talked about attending a school where the adults hit children and how it was the same school where some of his aunts and uncles went when they were his age:

> My worse school was P.S. XY 'cause they hit kids and my grandmother and my mother knew because they hit kids and my grandmother's sons and daughters went to that school. And that's a bad school.

He further recalled the details of why he brought a knife to school to protect himself against the threat of violence at the hands of his peers at his former school:

> A bunch of kids were trying to stab me at that school. I brought a knife to school with me, 'cause if a bunch of kids were going to stab me, then they were going to get stabbed back. So I went all the way to the first floor and I threw my knife under the stairwell and it was still there when I left because they never cleaned under there. I threw the knife in the steam room.

At his current school, Tyrone said he still did not feel safe and was hopeful about the prospect of going to a new school:

> I don't like school. But I know I'm going to do good in school at the next school I go to. My grandmother is going to pick my next school. She said she going to get me in a new school and I'm going to be all right.

In talking about his goals for the future, Tyrone made a connection to the lack of support he received from his teachers by drawing a distinction between what good teachers did and what bad teachers did:

> When I grow up, I'm going to do business; I'm going to make my own soda. I don't know any teachers that would talk to me about that. I don't know

what a good teacher does. Bad teachers do bad things, hit children, disrespect children, lie in front of their parents' face. I think they think like those parents is real dumb, letting their kids come to that school. They respect the parents, but they don't respect their children. Bad teachers don't care about...nobody. They care about themselves. I wrote a story about basketball, but none of the teachers asked me to, I just felt like doing it.

We talked about his awareness of his friends' aspirations for the future and he had this to say:

I don't know what none of my friends want to be when they get older...we never talk about that. We talk about what we going to do when we get home. We talk about when we get to high school and stuff. We going to have lockers and Freshmen Fridays, when the freshmen get jumped by the juniors and the seniors. I think they do that at every high school. My brother tells me when I get to high school; I'm going to have to be good.

He had this to say about relations between Blacks and Whites, and the bullies at his school:

White people are scared of Black people, but not all of them. I hate the White cops because they be stopping Black people just because they're Black. All White people are racist and I don't like them period. The Black kids in school, some of them can be bullies and think that you'll always be scared of them.

In talking about what he would say to his future son about the role school and education should play in his life, Tyrone shared:

If I had a son, I would tell him that he has to be good in school and maybe that I can be his role model. And he can probably be like me and play basketball and stuff. If he doesn't like basketball, I'd tell him to do a sport that he likes of his own. If he doesn't want that, then I'd tell him to do really good in school. If my son says education first and then basketball, or whatever, I'll be happy. Education should be first anyway. That's all right because I don't want to like take control of him.

Tyrone's schooling experiences thus far read like an indictment against many of the adults who were involved in the process. Still, glimmers of hope could be found in the support he now received from his stepfather, Joshua, and other members of his family outside of school.

Joshua the Father: A 23-year-old Store Clerk

Joshua's story addressed many issues that African American males encounter at all levels of school. He highlighted many changes that he felt were needed to turn the tide of success for African Americans. At the core of his argument was building a stronger relationship between teachers and their students. He discussed the role of family and the partnership that needed to be established between home and school.

Of his earliest memories of school, Joshua recalled playing with friends and having a pressure-free time:

> The first thing to come to mind is like a learning environment. A place where it's supposed to be a safe haven place where people are taught, you know. Earliest memories of school, I would have to say maybe pre-K. Playing with the toys, nap time, you know. I remember running around with my friends, I remember, you know, being introduced to homework and, you know, the concept of learning. The best thing, I guess it was no pressure.

Our conversation quickly shifted into the realities of what happened when one did not do well in school and the performance pressure that ensued as one became older:

> In the sense where, you know it's like if you don't do this, this or this, or if you mess up doing this, you're going to get held back or you're not going to be able to, you know, go to the school that you want to go to or, you know, just pressure. Like around high school. Maybe eighth grade, you know, people start getting letters on which high school they're going to. You always want to go to a good high school, you know. Some high schools, like some of the good high schools you have to take tests to get into the school. And then, you know, you want to make people proud and go to the best institutions so, you know, that's when really the pressure starts to hit you, like what are you going to do with life now?

Joshua talked about gym being the popular favorite among his peers and why:

> My favorite, let's see... I would probably say maybe like, most of the kids would probably say the same thing, gym was really like the best, the leisure time. Because when you're a kid, you know, you grow anxious, you want to move around a lot. When you're in class, they got you sitting down. The class was fun, but gym, you know they let you exercise and play basketball and you just really get some free time. The teachers were very nice, you know, some were strict, some stricter than others.

He shared his thoughts on his teachers and how they did or did not impact his growth as a young student:

> You do better with the ones that really, you know, were serious about teaching and serious about making you work and ones that took they're times, the ones that actually stayed after class, you know, the teachers who were really there for you. You just notice that a person goes out of they're way to help you learn something. Like where they just don't think of it like, "Oh, I'm just teaching." But if you tell them that you didn't get it and they sit down with you and show you step by step and explain the reason why you weren't getting it and just

show you everything. Not a lot. I could say in my whole time at school, maybe about three teachers were just really that good.

In thinking about his supportive teachers, one teacher in particular came to Joshua's mind:

> I can give you this example of this teacher, Mr. Slattery. Strict teacher, he was teaching at school when my mother was there, so good teacher. You miss a day, he'd, if you lived close to the area where he lived, he'd bring your homework and stuff to your house, knock on your door, go over your lesson with you. Say, even if you weren't doing as good as you were supposed to, he would take it above and beyond, you know, bring that education to you. And it's just something you'd never forget. As a kid, maybe it was like, "Oh man, my teacher's here at the door," but when you think about it, it was just like something I'll never forget. It's like; it's not that many that you feel that they didn't care but it almost feels that maybe for the time being they just were there, like it's just like a regular teacher.

He talked about the distinguishing characteristics of teachers who were truly invested in their students and their desire to teach everybody:

> You know, a person can see potential in another person so would think that that would, you know, motivate somebody to take the extra step with somebody because you want to see them succeed. Now, the teachers that weren't doing that, maybe they just didn't see it in the kids and maybe they just didn't want to go that extra mile, you know. And they might have done it for some other students and just not me. But it was just some teachers that stood out and took it on where I want to teach everybody.

Joshua went on to share his thoughts about the qualities he thought good teachers and good students should possess:

> Yes, yes, I think teachers should be very passionate about their work. You know, you're instructing the future of the society. So, above all, that's why sometimes, you know, teachers should be making the most money because you're the ones that are turning these kids into adults and adolescents and have them using their smarts. Now if you let a kid just breeze through just because you've seen a lot of kids like him with behavior problems, but you never get to the really core, he might go through his whole life in school like that. And I don't understand how there can be so many teachers who haven't made any impacts on kids, great impacts, where kids always remember the teachers that really sat there with me and really told me I have potential and told me I could do it and told me if I focused and reached out to my mother and called my father, you know, didn't care but just really wanted to educate you. Maybe some feel like I wasn't worth going the extra mile for.

He offered his take on what teachers needed to do to see beyond a child's behavior problems in school:

> You know, I understand that teachers don't really want to deal with, you know, a child with behavior problems who's constantly acting out. But if you can break down that defense mechanism that they put up, you get to a really good kid. Um, because, you know, maybe they just are not used to that, like getting shown love and respect and stuff like that, you know, coming from the projects and stuff.

Joshua specifically spoke about how African American males were raised to be tougher than others:

> Being a Black male, you're kind of brought up to be tough, like you have to be tougher than other people and you have to, you know, act certain ways in certain situations, you know, coming from where Black people really strive for education and then you look at people now and they treat it as if it's nothing. It was a point in time where education was so fortunate the Black people weren't taught, you know so to treat education like it was nothing when we worked so hard to get education, you know so when I see kids that slack off in school, even though I kinda did it, I still try to encourage them, you know, education is the key to success and your life.

He shared his remorse over some of the choices he made with his own behavior in school that he now saw their negative consequences:

> Totally, I wouldn't want to be the cool kid, you know, I wouldn't want to be the kid messing with all the girls and having fun because if you look at it in the long run, it's not worth it. Those who buckle down and handle their business, they experience more things than I would experience. It kind of makes you jealous because then you turn on the TV and there's a whole lot of college movies, there's movies that show you about this whole different life that you never get to experience.

Joshua continued to talk about his interest in teaching and a former inspirational teacher he had who ended up leaving the school because of tension with her colleagues:

> I'm actually kind of interested in teaching. No, 'cause I'm just like you can really make a difference there, like, you know, the teachers that were there for me, I'll never forget them. Like I had a teacher in high school, her name was Victoria. She was real down to earth and just really talked to us and she showed us the same level of respect that we showed her. She was White, a White teacher. But the thing about her that I didn't like was that the other teachers didn't like that about her, that she was so cool with the students. They didn't like that she really related to us and in the end that made her leave the school.

Joshua talked about what the system did to teachers who really tried to connect with their students:

> Sometimes they're forced out, like the teacher, Mr. Slattery, the one that came to my house, he was forced into retirement and you know, he really cried at the end because you can tell when somebody loves something for life and really wants to hold onto something, to deny a person that is just not right. Like, you know he taught generations and generations. Like my mother's generation, my generation and after my generation because I was long gone, he was still there.

Our conversation shifted to Joshua's thoughts on the impact of racism in schools and in society. He also discussed the influence of the media on the work ethic of African American male students:

> Well, if I understand, you consider that racism plays a part in it, but a Black male, he idolizes what he sees instead of what he knows. And to idolize what you see and what you have and anything that's on TV, that kind of takes the focus off school. Like, you know, there are not a lot of rappers with college degrees, who would even glorify a college degree and it shouldn't be like that. You know, why can't smart men be rappers just because it's the career that they chose? You know, like Black people, we have this fantasy that education is just something that, you know, you can get an education, but then there's people who have made it without education. Like you can sit back and you can say, "Well, the president had a C average." Well, there's a lot of Black kids with C averages, you know, and that's hard to maintain a C average. I think people like to take the easy way and in school, there's never an easy way. People don't really like to work for stuff, people like things handed out to them. Because when you watch stuff on TV, it's like instantaneous, they made a song and instantaneous, they got millions and they're running around the globe now.

Joshua shared his opinion of the seeming fascination of young African American males with wanting to become professional basketball players:

> Basketball, yeah, basketball has saved a lot of Black kids, saved, and it's really doing wonders, you know, for a sport to really come in and help a community, but there still has to be a foundation behind it, some type of structure. Because you can go around basketball and be so good that your talent outshadows your academic levels and a kid like that might get a pass, you know, might get a pass with some grades, with a fail or, you know, just pick up and go straight to the NBA and doesn't even finish school. That's what people see, when their reality sets in, they look at it like, "Well, I've got two options. I can rap or I can go play basketball." But it's never an option that "I can work hard, start my own business and become a self-made man."

I asked Joshua what advice he would give to African American boys about other options, besides sports, they should consider for their futures:

The message I would give them is just you can be anything; if you apply yourself, you can really be anything, like nothing is impossible. And it's so amazing to me that you can really sit back and think of it and really say that nothing impossible, you can achieve anything that you really put your mind to, nothing is impossible. And that's the message that I just really want to show, like "Yeah, you might want to be a basketball player, but I would try to see if you want to be a doctor to save lives too and you'll make money, if you might want to be a teacher." If you let people know that they can do anything and they really believe that they can do anything, they're going to do whatever they're really inspired to do. Just by showing them.

Joshua believed that the images presented to African American males did not inspire them to invest in education:

Like, if you have to go pick up Black men magazines and, okay, because if we start glorifying these other smart Black people who are doing things, it shows you that it is not just two options for them and that you really can be anything that you put your mind to. You know, if instead of hanging up pictures of Michael Jordan, if we hang up pictures of Frederick Douglass and show them. You see, because I don't think that people understand how important education is and how us as a Black people, we weren't being taught, like back in the days when we were slaves and stuff like that, how education was a privilege that we weren't receiving any benefits from and how people had to teach themselves and how you had to hide the fact that you were smart, you know. They need to see that so they can appreciate education because it's really something that you need to appreciate.

Joshua talked about the perception that many African American students had about not wanting to show that academics matter and the influence of what they saw in their own communities:

It's definitely not slavery but, you know, they try to make it look like being smart is just not cool, you know, and all kids want to be cool, but when you're in a place where being smart is not cool, people try to hide it. And if you hide it for long enough, sooner or later, you'll really be that person that, you know, you were hiding behind. If we glorify more smart kids, if we have more spelling bees, more contests, and just reward Black people more for being smart, you know scholarships and programs, you know things that glorify smarter kids and smarter Black kids, then there will be smarter Black kids. Because of the people that are out there on the corners, you know, the people that are going to be out there forever, you know, making them look like this is the only step for them.

He also shared his thoughts around role models for people living in low-income areas:

97

People believe in more things that they see than what they hear. They need to know that not a lot of people aren't going to make it out of the ghetto unless successful people who have come back and show people that they made it. Like, you know, if you start a company, come back to where you were, I know you might not want to deal with these people, get them jobs, give them chances to better themselves. If you come back and show people a different way, you know, "I know they're over there doing it this way, but look how I did it." You can pull a couple more out with you. And if they went out and did the same exact thing, they could pull a couple more out with them and if it keeps going like that, eventually, everyone. Yeah, and some people feel that that's the way you gain success, like you can't gain success unless you know somebody. You know, they do say it a lot, it's not what you know but really who you know, but you have to look at is it works in the same way. But it's a lot easier if you come into your community and you bring in your old friends, you know, bring in the people that you grew up with and the people that you want to see, you know, better themselves.

Even in the example Joshua provided for the mentoring model he described, safety became an issue to consider:

People will put up their wall, barrier because they think it's not safe, you know this might happen. If you show them, you know, "This is a safe way." You have to be there with them, though, like, if you show a person—like someone told me this, if you and a friend go fishing, he can eat for that night, but if you teach him how to fish, he can eat for the rest of his life.

Joshua shared with me how his father used to discuss with him the importance of school, but he did not fully digest the value of what he was saying at the time:

He talked to me about school, you know, that education is very important and that messing up in school won't get you anywhere. But sometimes it just doesn't sink in at the time, where, you know, I listen to everything he was saying to me now. But at the time I just wasn't really focused on that.

He described the prescriptive nature of what the majority of his classrooms were like and the type of teacher he would be:

Yeah, like you go into the class and it was set up with desks in rows, everyone was assigned a seat. You know, some classes had the tables that were connected together, four people. Everyone was assigned seats; we did work from worksheets and workbooks. You know, it's not something that grips your attention like a teacher who takes initiative and plans out a lesson and really says, "You know what? Well, we're going to have fun with this and they're going to learn." That's the type of teacher that I would like to be. You know, someone who sits there and says, "Okay, if we do this, I know it's something everyone will have fun with and it's education too." The workbooks, you know, read this page, okay, and then you know, the individual work. The teacher says, you know, "Do chapter four and chapter five, then do the questions at the end and everybody raise your hand when you finish." That there's no effort in it, like it's just textbook.

According to Joshua, science was his favorite subject and this was how he described his experiences with it in school:

You know, I like science, it's my favorite subject, I like science because you actually did what you were talking about. You know, when you were talking about the carbons and hydrogen, you actually got in there with your hands and you know, we dissected frogs, we dissected pigs. So you really were in to the stuff that you did. Yeah, it was like knowledge, but then again it was real. Because it was brought right to you and you didn't only see it, you felt it. Because it's like this is real, okay. Because I can tell you something so many times, "Okay, this is the way to do it, this is the way to do it." But if you've never seen the way to do it—yeah, and if you've never experienced it, you can just think like, "Ah well, that might be the way but I don't think that's the way".

He talked about how students may be resistant to new information in school and what teachers needed to do to help them grow as learners:

Yeah, a lot of kids think that, "Like, oh, it's not going to help me in life." Well, honestly, they need to know not to feel sorry for them. Don't feel sorry because "Oh, he's a Black kid and he's not really learning." No. You need to treat them as if you would teach your child. You know, people can tell when something's genuine, you know, and when you're really teaching and it's from your heart and you really care about people. You know, people can sense that and people can sense when you're just going along, "lalalala," and that might turn the kid away from you, you know. I guarantee it, if you try your hardest with all your students, there wouldn't be one who just didn't get it or who just stopped showing up to class. If you reached out to every last one of them and showed them every time, I understand when people say, "It should be smaller classes and smaller schools," but it's not necessarily that. It's the teaching and it starts with the teaching. You might have a thousand students and you have to find a way to teach, you have to find a way to make something spark in a thousand students. It's just what you have to do. When a teacher reaches out to a thousand students, that's something really good. And it's something that they can appreciate too and I know it just makes you feel some type of way, at the end of the day where, you know, you put your all into your education and into your school.

This is how Joshua responded to the societal perception that African American boys lacked male role models. He specifically referenced basketball players and what they could do to shine a light on the value of education to the boys who looked up to them:

> Of course, they have male role models, they have so many. Like, how many Black athletes are there? And for a Black athlete just to come on and say "Education is the key." Yeah, "Don't be like me." Just because you're playing doesn't mean you have to shut down your education. You can get your degree online, there are so many ways to learn so, like you can't really cut yourself off to that, like there's a lot of Black role models out there, you know, that nobody knows about, you know. You just have to shine some light on them.

Joshua went on to talk about the responsibility of parents in supporting their children:

> You know, things I would do different, I would just sit down with my son, do the work with him, try not to get too uptight, because a lot of men, they get caught up in their own things and you look like you don't have time for your son to sit down and do work with him. Some parents are like that, you know if they had a bad day at the office and they come home and they're cranky so your kid doesn't want to go to you and, you know, ask about that. You have to make it seem like for their education, you have to go above and beyond and you know really sit there and check the homework and correct it with them, you know. Nine out of ten times if you sit there with the child, you might learn something. I do with Tyrone.

He shared his thoughts on the lack of emotional investment that he believed happened in the high school environment:

> You know, I remember elementary school teachers said she'll call your mother, you straighten right up. You start sitting up, start reading, I remember that. But when you get to high school it's like…they just need to act like they love their students, like it's a different environment from elementary school and then high school. Elementary school is like sheltered, you feel loved, like some of these high schools, they're so big that kids just slip through the system unseen, you know.

Joshua offered some structural changes that might help children succeed in school:

> But if it takes hiring more teachers, then maybe you want to hire more teachers. If it takes having a teaching assistant in the class where he's working this side and he's working this side, if that's what it takes, then that's what it takes. Like, there are people out there who are willing to help these kids. So why should they not be able to help. If you could just come in and just speak about what you've been through and how education has impacted you, you might touch one kid. If you touch one kid out of forty kids, then he might turn another kid around, this is what I'm looking at.

Joshua reflected on his own poor choices in school in comparison to his peers that managed to make it to college:

He might turn his friends, like, people don't think that you can really make a big difference as one person, but you really can. Yeah, I had a whole variety of friends. It made me mad when I saw some of my friends moving on to college and stuff and I wasn't. And these are the friends who did the same things I did; played around the same ways I did, but just went at it differently when it came about their schoolwork. Like, just make sure they got their homework done. Yeah, but you know, just made sure they got their homework done, made sure that when they were in class that they were focusing and still learning, and still passing tests. That kind of made me look at myself like, you know, how did I let myself get into this situation and they're going on? And it's like we were doing the same thing, you know, all the times we were joking but they did something different. Yeah.

For Joshua, racism in society continued to impact the educational and societal outcomes for African American males:

I think that a Black male is very dangerous for the simple fact that he has the whole world at his hands and he can do anything he wants to do. So a Black man in a White world, it's very dangerous because they don't want to, you know, a lot of Black men succeed, so I think the more knowledge you have, the more dangerous you are. The smarter you are and the more that you know that they don't know, you know, that's when you start to become a threat because of what you know. Racism is in the background. It's not as much as it was at first, but it still plays a role, it still really plays a role.

In addition, he commented on the negative impact of tracking in school and suggested that classrooms be purposefully designed to have mixed ability grouping, so that students can help each other learn:

By just getting the word out there, getting the message. Glorifying smart kids, not just the smart Black kids but the smart kids and putting the smart ones in the class with the dumb ones so they can teach them. You know, if you have a whole class full of dumb kids, and that's how they did it sometimes, they'll separate kids. Like in elementary school, they had fourth/fifth graders, like the class had some fourth graders and it'll be some fifth graders and some of them were, you know, a little bit slower. But what you need to do is place those kids with the smart kids, let them work together, get them to do work together, pair them off. Yeah, why would you have a class full of dumb people, why would that be an agenda to break up these students? "Well, these students are not as smart as these students and these students have a behavior problem and all of that."

He shared this observation about how African Americans can change children's perceptions that education is not cool:

Like, I really think Black people can make smartness look cool, you know. Showcase them, showing people, you know let's through some of these rappers or entertainers on game shows, you know, these shows like Jeopardy or, what show as I watching? Mos Def was up there and he was talking about politics and stuff like that and we need to see more stuff like that.... You know, that's what I said, you put them on these smart game shows and showcase them to where they see like it's not, you know, whack to be smart. It's cool.

Another change Joshua suggested based on his own schooling was to change the texts used in schools to be more reflective of the contributions of African Americans to society:

Yeah, you look in a textbook, it's about five hundred pages, and it may have only three to four chapters about African American history, in a book of five hundred pages and it only has three or four chapters of African American history, just to balance it out, just to show that—not good quality. Yeah, Black people were slaves. Yeah, Martin Luther King, Malcolm X, some Black people did a couple of things, you know. They just never really focused and never really highlighted the things that we've done.

He remembered his own music class and how it underrepresented the contributions of African Americans in various musical genres:

Especially, like in music, in music class. They don't go to the root of where a lot of this music really came from, you know, the beginning of rock and roll, jazz and to the bottom to where all this stuff really came from nine out of ten times. But when you get down to the very bottom of where it first originated and nobody glorifies that.

In our last conversation, Joshua offered this passionate argument about the importance of teachers seeing the overall value of the work that they did:

I just want to make a point that teachers, man, teachers are really, they're just really everything. You know, we don't treat them as if they are everything, a law should be added that at one point of your life you're going to have to be a teacher and you're going to have to teach somebody something. Because teachers, they really need to be glorified for what they do and what they really are. And you know, they have to realize what comes with being a teacher, you have to think about the responsibility that comes with teaching, the responsibility of having, you know, this kid's future in their hands. Just by enlightening, just by words, you know words spark up conversations that can ignite someone's soul. So just by talking to somebody and just by, you know, understanding them and trying to get to the core of their problem. Like, if I could just see all the teachers doing that, just doing that one thing, a lot of change.

While Joshua did not go to college, many of the points he has made were reiterated and expanded upon by his cousin, Larry, who did graduate from college.

Larry the Cousin: A 23-year-old College Student

Larry had much to say about his experiences in school. He identified himself as a good student. He did not grow up with his father in the home, but he was in constant contact with him growing up and attributed much of his academic success to his family. His talked up the impact of where he grew up:

> I wouldn't say I grew up in a rough neighborhood, but if I grew up on the other side of the tracks, there would have been a better opportunity for me to learn advance skills. Whatever the case may be, but I definitely was given what I needed to be successful…but what you don't have you try to find a way to get it.

For Larry, the support he received from his family and his teachers helped him with school:

> I think my family was the biggest piece of that. If you don't have what you need in the classroom, you have an uncle or a brother, or a cousin that can get it at least halfway there. In school I had a lot of great teachers. I was blessed to be a good student. If I did have a problem learning something, the teachers didn't mind pulling me aside to help me with extra time in class or after class to make sure I got what I needed. I definitely think it benefits the student to have a good family structure as well.

He also talked about what he contributed to the equation when he described himself as a young student: "I was always outgoing, always wanted to participate, I made good grades because I was willing to do the work. I was mature at an early age and I think that played in my favor." He spoke specifically about his relationship with his father and the lessons he has learned from him over the years:

> I had a very good relationship with my father, he's always been the one that lead by example and always challenged me and I used to hate it. Because if you didn't understand something, you sat at the table until you got it. You could cry your eyes out, but you got yourself together. You sat there until you learned the skills that you needed to learn.

As a parent, Larry said that his father's parenting style was partially based on his own life experiences and partially "trial and error":

> He knew that the world was going to be tough and he knew that I was going to have to have a backbone to succeed. He had to learn through trial and error because there wasn't someone there to guide him through it all. He wanted to be there for me to make sure I had the resources, the knowledge…that I wasn't going to be afraid of work.

Of his relationship with his early teachers, he described his personal connection with them:

My first grade teacher, I loved her. I did a lot of plays; she was always in the front cheering me on. I kept in contact with her over the years. When I went to college she gave me a huge basket of things. People were like, "You still talk to your first grade teacher?" and I was like, "Doesn't everybody?" I think that shows how I was as a student, I never want to burn a bridge with anyone." For second and third grade, I had the same teacher; she helped me develop my verbal and writing skills. During that time I really flourished as a student.

Larry remembered his seventh grade science teacher and the impression she made on him at the time:

My seventh grade science teacher, she loved science so much that you kind of sort of loved it too. Because she loved it. You didn't know why. I think she was the first person I met that she was really in love with what she was doing.

He commented on what he thought was happening in the minds of teachers who were not invested in their students and what they were missing:

I think a lot of teachers feel like I have my objectives that I have to teach and if I do my objectives, well, then, that's all I have to do. When you're going to influence someone's life, it's more than your objectives. It's actually getting in to see about the well-being of your students because you see them on a daily basis. Some people come from broken homes, some people don't have that foundation. So you meet your objectives, but you go beyond that to make sure your students have that foundation. Not just from the fundamentals, but the whole well being to be successful. I think a lot of teachers miss that piece.

We discussed college and Larry shared how he had to navigate that situation on his own because he did not really have family to help him with that. He noted making mistakes along the way, but eventually he was able to move through college successfully. Our conversation shifted to the educational situation facing African American boys today. He had much to say on this topic:

The trend didn't start yesterday, it wasn't something where we went to sleep and woke up and said, "Hey, we have a lot of Black people in jail, it's a lot of Black males dropping out of high school." I think we've seen it for a very long time; no one has really stepped up to take responsibility to do something about it…. I think a lot of people just left it up to the school system to teach what was needed…. You have a lot of intelligent thugs out there…. How you apply what you get at school, you get that at home.

Larry commented on the notion of a lack of African American male role models and hyper-masculinity that was attributed to young African American males in school:

My father was still active even though my parents weren't together. You need both parents even if they don't live together…. I don't think our culture was responsible for that hyper-masculinity piece. I really think the media has a lot to do with that. And it's been going on for a very long time. Being a hyper-masculine male gets you where? Peers and TV are telling the stories…it's being seen as real to a lot of Black people in society.

In our last conversation, Larry offered this advice to young African American males:

> You have to work twice as hard. Nothing's going to be given to you. There's going to be challenges. You have to be used to being the representation for your community. Embrace that; understand that everyone isn't after you. You don't always have to be defensive. You don't always have to respond…. And reach out to others once you get to that point where you have made it, go back and help show someone else how.

Larry's story was one of resiliency and belief in education. His trajectory was very different than his cousin's, Joshua. He made connections with his teacher and had the support of his grandmother, whom he called a survivor, and his parents. The role of family was clearly highlighted in his schooling experiences. Moving forward five decades in age, we see that his advice to young African American males was echoed and expanded on in 73-year-old Jacob's story of his schooling experiences.

Jacob the Great-Grandfather: Retired Truck Driver

Jacob's story provides a historic overview of the educational issues not only in the Freeman family but in the African American community. The value of education was clear for him, but there was also a sense of remorse over the mistakes of his generation in providing a strong educational and community foundation for the next generation. As a result of his awareness and experiences, Jacob suggested a variety of areas such as strengthening the community, bolstering familial bonds; and returning to core values that have sustained African Americans in the past, and that need to be addressed to bring positive educational outcomes for African American males.

Jacob began to share the story of his schooling in the segregated South in the 1950s:

> My school history…when I was going to school, like in '50, '51-2-3, when I was going to high school. You find at that stage of life or that, children were more interested in school at that time. It was before that my older brothers and sisters and things they didn't have the opportunity to go to school. You know they worked in the farm. People realized that, my generation came along, what school was all about. How it will help the progress of a new generation, that it was just all entirely different. And when we went to school, we went to school really to learn up until twelfth grade, that's as far as my generation was really able to go. Or financially able to go, I should say. Even if you had, it wasn't all these grants and things available for you.

He talked about the harsh realities of being in the South and not being able to afford to go to college, regardless of how high one's grades were in that era:

105

So your parents by always working, you know, some of them were sharecroppers. Even my grandmother, she had her own farm at the time but still hadn't acquired no money, a lot of money, you know, things of that nature. So what you got you had to work for. You had to put in the labor for it; we just didn't have no money to go to college. And like me, for example, I was making As and Bs and Cs in high school. And I say I would left with maybe a B+ average. And the opportunity was there you couldn't—so what you do, you go out for the big city. Find a job that would pay more money and stuff. It was mostly like being in the South because other people you know, the car industry, things like Detroit and all that really began to flourish at that time and Black men did have a much better job. And when you were in a certain section of the United States that you had that availability to go to school and to better yourself.

Jacob explained that people left the South in pursuit of better finances and with that came more access to furthering their education:

That's why it took us Southern people longer to gravitate towards education because they did not have the finances. Southerners moved into cities because of low income, they were looking for higher income and better opportunities. So what they did they left the country, or whatever you want to call it, but they left in order to get a better job that paid more. The idea was to have your kids could have a better opportunity, a better chance than you had. Most of the people I graduated with, they was, I would say very good students. And a lot of them should go to college but the only reason they didn't go was that they wasn't financially able to go to college. But as far having good grades, they had good grades.

Jacob shared his memories of elementary school in a one-room schoolhouse serving multiple grades at one time:

I remember going to elementary school, what we called kindergarten; we had primary school for five years. We went to school when we was five years old for one year and they called it kindergarten, but a we went to a country school. You had to walk three miles to go to school. You didn't have a bus at the time. Then by the time, that was for up until eighth grade. See that school covered up until eighth grade. Everybody in the neighborhood or in the community would go to that school.

He went into further detail about the structure of having three teachers, including the principal, who taught about one hundred children from the neighborhood:

Well, I tell you, you had three teachers, that's including the principal. The principal taught, too. And in the classroom you may have as high as forty-five people. You had three teachers, in the neighborhood, teaching at least ninety to a hundred kids. And you had to teach from the first grade till eighth grade, before you could go to high school. And after you graduated from the eighth grade you went to high and that's from the ninth thru the twelfth.

He discussed the logistics involved with having one school bus serving multiple sections of town and the impact on the beginning and ending of the school day:

We lived back off the highway and they had a school bus at the time that goes to the high school only. And they had to be there like eight o'clock in the morning. You catch the bus and go there. You had to leave at two o'clock in the afternoon in order to service the many neighborhoods. Now you talking about sections, you know, one small town, with ten different sections. Just one school bus going to these different sections. It take two and a half hours just to collect everybody. The same for dropping off in the afternoon, so you have to always leave school a half an hour early, 'cause 2:30 you had to leave, and school turn out at three but you had to leave early 'cause you caught the bus.

According to Jacob, all of his teachers were good teachers and they were biracial. He mentioned how their access to education was based on the fairness of their skin color:

We had all Black teachers, Mr. Bonds was the principal and he was half and half. And they really go by lightness and stuff like that, you know, we had twenty teachers at the high school. The more fair you were, it seemed like the better opportunity you had. Like the principal and all the teachers were half White. The principal's sister taught English. She could have graduated from Harvard 'cause she knew a lot. We had the regular teachers that anybody else would have had. We had an algebra teacher, a chemistry teacher, and a biology teacher. We had some excellent teachers.

This is how he described the foundation for acceptable behavior at his high school:

They had discipline, the school itself, you weren't allowed to talk loud and run over everybody or anything of that nature. You had a code of honor, a code of ethics. No uniforms, you wore what you could have.

Jacob talked about life as a teenager and the popular inexpensive power lunch:

Of course, everybody when you're at that stage of the game, that stage of life, things begin to change a little bit. You had a little more clothes and things of that nature, but you still weren't up to par like the normal people—you still didn't have that money. You still had to pay so much for lunch, twenty cents for lunch and stuff like that. And still I say fifty percent of the kids that went to high school, they didn't eat because they didn't have the twenty cents a day. They had to run to the store and get a Pepsi Cola and a bun—that was the famous thing. A big sugar bun and that was your energy to keep you going until you got home.

Jacob talked about his relationship to his siblings and their educational journeys:

> There were eight of us six boys and two girls. When I went high school, my sister Lois, she was ahead of me, she didn't finish the last year. She got married so she didn't complete high school. She was very good in school, a good writer and things of that nature. She was an excellent writer and knew a lot about decorating and things of that nature. She always knew decorating. Victor, my brother, he went to high school, four grades behind me, so by the time I graduated, then he was going to school. Now, he and Fredrick went to school together. Victor was very good in high school, he kept his grades and things up and Fredrick, he was the youngest one. I done left home by this time you know, by the time he went to high school. I left home, Fredrick he did well too. First when I left home, I was graduating when I was eighteen and then I went to New York to live with my brother David. He was already there, he was the oldest, and naturally like everybody you want a job, you look for a job. I went to the Air Force after about a year. I volunteered for the Air Force. Me and Lois was always tight because we grew up together, we were like twins, then Victor come, you know, you used to love all your brothers and sisters.

Jacob mentioned the familial support structures that were put in place to support raising children while his parents worked up North.

> I know very little about my grandfather, my grandfather on my father's side I never knew, he passed away when he was thirty-five years old. My father had to raise most of the kids with his brother. They had to do a lot of work, they don't tell you a lot of details, they don't tell you what he died from. My father, he worked hard, and my grandmother, we lived on a farm and we had to do work ourselves, you know. My father left and he went up North and he was working on the railroad for a long time. He was up north working and we was working on a farm with our grandmother. He'd come down about four or five times a year, he'd come in the summers for maybe two weeks and stuff like that. That went on until Lois was born—see, Lois was born in the North and, see; I was born in the South. My mother was up North with my father, and my grandmother was doing most of the raising us. She had a big house.

This is how he described his grandmother who raised him and his siblings on their farm:

> Oh, my grandmother, she was a very stern lady and a very learned lady. She went to eighth grade, she had about an eighth grade education, but you would say she went to college because she could read anything you could imagine. She was more than college material, my grandmother was. She was very sharp and she was very stern, you know, she wouldn't let nobody walk over her or tell her anything. Especially when she thought she was right. She raised us

'cause she only had one daughter, that was my mother and no other kids. She felt like we was her kids, too and that's the way she raised us.

Jacob shared the details of growing up during a time of open racism in the South and spoke of a friendship that could not withstand its destructive nature:

We never experienced cross burnings and stuff like that, but we knew White people who was very racist. They come in all types and forms, you know. I'll tell you a good example: when we came out to the highway where we lived at there was a country store. We called it a country store. And in that store, it was ran by Whites, the Odwell family, and her husband was a real nice man. But she was very prejudice, very prejudice, when I say prejudice, she was so prejudice until if you got close to her she'd turn very red. She change her whole complexion and everything, you could see it within her. And then she had one kid named Phil. And he used to come down, we lived on the riverfront, by the way, and he used to come down and play with me all the time. He used to love me, like we loved one another, but she didn't want him to really play with me, or things of that nature. There's a Southern mentality, of where you can go and where you can't you learn that from your fore-parents. The thing is mostly you learned how not to do these things because they easily want to jail you or to fine you for some reason out of the ordinary. They look for things of that nature. They feel like they were superior to you and you weren't.

In Jacob's opinion, racism still existed but just manifested itself in a different form:

No, it hasn't changed. The concept has changed. Today it's a different form of integration, segregation and all that kind of thing. Today people say one thing with their lips and do things behind your back. Now things are just not out in the open no more, it's behind closed doors, but it really goes on in a lot of cases that it's still the same old joke. Back then, it was honest, more honest when it was out in the open, because you knew where you stand. Now, you don't know where you stand. You don't know who's stabbing you. You know, the person next to you is saying one thing and doing another. They're waiting on an opportunity to do this to you, you know. Say I want to stab you bad, but I'll wait until the opportunity come, first mistake you make, you know, Bam!

Jacob offered this explanation of generational shifts in African Americans' understanding of the value of education as more people began to go to school and gain greater access to better employment:

Well, that's all entirely different than when I was brought up. You see, generations began to change when people began to learn more book learning. And when you learn more in the book way, you learn about life. You read more. Now when I came along I knew my children, I gave them the best opportunity that I can because I know what's out there, I know what the world is about today. And it was about, back then, you have to have an education. You see, when I came along, you have to finish high school, that was the idea. If you finish high school, you see, you get a better job, you get a city job and all kinds of jobs of that nature.

Once his generation began to have children, they set their sights higher for their children's education, but Jacob said they were still behind their White peers:

And then when I came along by knowing all this and then by working in better establishments, you see, and then you learned that your kids need to go to college. Because they was phasing out high school, you know, each generation the White folks want to stay one step ahead of you. So now when I came along a high school diploma was a great thing and then they see that so many Black people have a high school diploma. And see then the advancement comes and they see you must go to college. Now they send all their kids to college, they come for the good jobs again because now the good jobs are moving up.

Even with more African Americans having access to college education than his generation, Jacob continued to see the legacy of racism being passed on:

The moment you got to college, you need special education or you need to advance in this particular thing, major in this, you know, or a computer is the great thing if you go to college and you may go to college for five or six years and still don't get the job that you qualified to do, you know. And they find ways to send their kids, and that's because my father has been there the whole time. You see the White man, his father has been there and he has worked his way up all the time and he has schemed on you to keep you down all the time. You see he never want you to reach the pedestal that he's at, you see, he don't want you on that level.

Jacob expanded on his previous comment by detailing the White racist mentality that feeds the machine of systemic racism in this country:

But now it gets so close, you see you was a hundreds of years behind, you couldn't read six hundred years ago. You couldn't read or write. It was against the law for you. See now you caught up too fast for him, he's still angry with you. He still don't appreciate that, you know. He still don't want you to be president of a university, he don't like that too good, you know. He don't like that too well. You [he] feel like well I'm the epitome of education, I'm the epitome of everything that's running this country because this is my country. You know when they say this *my* country. They mean that really down deep in their hearts, they mean that. So I don't know if that statement will ever get out of them. It'll always be there.

Jacob talked about education as having the power to break the down systemic racism and prejudice of those who have historically been in positions of power, and how African Americans have known this for a long time:

And they show you how to make fast money and all this kind of stuff. That's something to slow you down, and that's why I say it's so hard to get around the system, the system is made, geared all the ways toward you to hold you back. It's instilled within your heart, when they say prejudice, it's not so much one individual being prejudice, but the group themselves being prejudice. The whole system was geared towards prejudice from day one. I'm supported, I'm God, you know. And some will come out and tell you that directly, you know. That's the way it's always going to be. It's only one way to break the system… it's education, you know. And that's the only way and we been right on that. It's a lot of things we been wrong on. On that we been right.

Jacob offered a powerful metaphor of the links of a chain to describe the breakdown that has happened in the African American community, which he attributed to purposefully-placed obstacles within society:

We reached a point where we was advancing fast. Now they throw so many obstacles in our way until it slowed us down. I think we're at a period now where we slowed down a lot from obstacles that he had thrown in our way. Drugs, schools don't care, bringing out silly styles, everything to please you; he working on you. You see, he's sizing you up and he figures you out and then he goes to the weakest link. And when you go to the weakest link that breaks the chain. The strongest link don't break the chain. It's the weakest link and so he always throwing something there for you. If you was really trying to help, you wouldn't go the weakest link, you'd go to the strongest link and then you take that strong link and then you build, you put another strong link with it. Keep building like that, that's what you do and you try to omit the weakest link, you try to through him out 'cause he going to break.

From Jacob's perspective, athletes are not the best role models for African American boys because they tend to be weak academic role models:

To help African American, Black boys, we need a lot of role models. We don't need no athlete to be a role model, because he's not there, he hasn't advanced far enough himself. All he knows how to do is, he got a terrific body and he doesn't have that terrific mind. You see, you need people that look like a wimp that has a good mind that can come out in help. But you have to deal with each family, 'cause this family thing has gone bust a little bit, you know.

He went on to discuss the importance of family, especially extended family as a means of survival in the African American community and not money:

My brothers and sisters always brought our families together; we spent time together as one big family. You know that's why it's so many people they don't survive. I don't care about how much money you make, money isn't an important thing in life, no, not the most important thing in life. Love is the most important thing in life, love…love one another. Be godly.

111

Jacob talked about the role of African American male teachers and their responsibility to create a family-like classroom environment to impact the lives of their students positively:

> So much of our culture is based on, if I didn't experience it, if I didn't see it, then I don't believe it. You have to get young children to believe in you. You the first father figure they meet. It's like an usher at the door, you the first one that they meet. And it's your impression, therefore when you lecture to them, you have to show them love, kindness, that they never had. You have to show them something because they're looking for something, a sign. Family, the class has got be like a family, that's what you have to show them. That way it's not just about learning from one person, you're learning from everybody in that family. You can get a few kids to believe in you, you know it's like a chain, one person catch on and then another person. Then the kids without families at home will eventually say you taught them something that I never knew before.

Jacob further talked about shared responsibility in addressing the problems that continue to plague our schools:

> See, the problems come because it's all our responsibilities. We waited to long to deal with, the professors and everything, waited to long. See, it's not one person to blame, see, it's all of us to blame. It's all of our responsibility to work on it together. See, you cannot go in the classroom and do and fulfill everything in there. You cannot do it to save your life!

He shared the educational aspirations of previous generations and the underlying investment in the education of African American children that seems to have become lost over time:

> Our father, he thought of having a better education, a better environment for us. You know a better education so that we could have the knowledge to go out and gain, what we called the valuable things in life; you know, the new car, the new house. And so he thought that if he gave us the opportunity to send us to school that we would eventually grow into having a better life. For our kids, when our kids came along, most parents they overdid it, you know, they forgot where they came from. And they forgot what they were taught; you know you were always taught about God and Christ. That's just like wearing a pair of shoes, that was brought up in you daily, you know, you wore that. And when young people got out of line, older people would quickly get you right back in line. And they didn't mind doing it 'cause that's just the way it worked. And that was a good life to a certain extent. It wasn't a bad life like people said; it was a good life to a certain extent because everybody you know cared about one another in that neighborhood. Everybody cared, they may talk about one another, when things came down everybody cared.

For Jacob, when the focus of his generation shifted to securing material wealth over educational wealth, that was when things began to break down:

> When the next generation came along, naturally college was the most important thing in our lives, 'cause you already had a knowledge of going to church. But you didn't have that financial burden that we had. See, we spoiled our kids, that generation, because we gave you things that we never had. Not the true moral things that we need to sustain us, we gave them luxury things, everything that we thought they needed we give them. Out charging sneakers, a hundred dollars, immature things, that's what we did. And that ruined the society, half of it, some made advancements. Some gained knowledge, some took advantage—crybabies, oh, I never had this and they grab and try to get more of the wrong things, see, they went the other way.

He shared his concern for his grandson's generation, with the lure of the streets and the power of prayer and community to bring needed change:

> I don't know what to hope for my grandson's generation that looked like it lost. Our whole thing, we have to come back to basics, you know you have to continue to understand, that young men today need a father. So you don't find a father in the street, you find a monster—he can say what he wants, he's not out there in the street. You can go to church, but church no longer, it's not enough. It's enough if you really got involved, but everybody don't get involved with church. It's so many other social events that they can apply today and that's what we need. We need to get back to basics. It's so hard to get the community to look out for each other, now it's getting the community to solve the problem without being vindicated by anybody. So we keep trying, make sure we go to the lord and pray, prayer changes things for everybody. You see on that day in time, sometimes my father, he brought us together and prayed on Sunday morning.

Jacob suggested that teachers and African American fathers should build a stronger bond to bring change in educational outcomes for children:

> Everybody these days got an education, they should just get together, like Black fathers just get together and have a convention and have teachers there to *teach them* what it's all about and this way, see it will trickle down.

He pointed out that government funding and big money alone will not solve the problems plaguing our schools; rather, changes need to happen in the fabric of society:

> And see waiting on the government to trickle you some money down, this will trickle down much faster, so then it's not about the money. It's about people. Money is what ruined a lot of people, they become about the love of money— they think money can by everything. People think they can buy, get out of jail,

long as you got money. You see that with these ball players nowadays, they get their millions of dollars and high society. They think they've jumped through to another category, see it's not true, society don't want you there.

Jacob suggested that African Americans need to consider building structures outside of the parameters of existing society to model what society needs to do:

If you leave that society alone and build one of your own you'd be much better off because that society always have put a stumbling block in your way. See, you build your own and then they'll recognize it, see, that's the only solution that I see. I think my family truthfully has been blessed only by God and it's not so much of our doing, but when you got something in you, something's going to come out. When you don't have nothing in you, well, then, nothing will come out, you see it's who you associate with. If you associate in the street, then the street going to come out in you. If you associate with church, then the church going to come out of you. If you associate within education with teachers, than that's what's going to come out of you.

Jacob's story offered a painful account of dealing with racism in the South to racism as it stands today. His reflection on his schooling experiences contained elements of the schooling experiences of all of the younger Freeman males. Jacob was able to envision what areas needed to be addressed to improve the educational outcomes of African American males now and in the future.

A number of similar and new themes emerged from this family's stories. These themes connect the three individual families to a commonality of lived experiences over a span of 63 years. Specifically, four major thematic categories emerged from the three family stories, which constituted the data for this study. The themes within each category were analyzed and are discussed next in Chapter VIII. Emerging from the thematic analysis was the metatheme of collective achievement.

CONNECTING THE COLLECTIVE

My study intended to address the missing voices of African American males in the literature by engaging with African American males from the same family unit across generations through qualitative interviews and observations in their homes and communities. According to Holstein and Gubrium (1995), "Active interview data are analyzed to show the dynamic interrelatedness of the what and the how.... the focus is as much on the assembly process (by both respondent and researcher) as on what is assembled" (p. 79). Data from the field log, interviews, and observations were analyzed to identify patterns, themes, metathemes, and unique cases that related to my research topic, provided answers to my research questions, and suggested further issues and questions to consider (Ely et al., 1991, p. 151).

In creating a road map to analyze the data generated in this study, themes and metathemes were instrumental in interpreting these data. A theme is a "statement of meaning" that can be found running through most of the data or it can be derived from more specific data surrounding a significant emotional or factual event. Metathemes are "major constructs that highlight overarching issues in a study which may be considered against extant literature and experience" (Ely et al., 1997, p. 206). Certain pieces of data that seemed to fall in stark contrast to the rest were analyzed to understand the meaning behind their uniqueness.

My analysis of the data revealed four important intergenerational-thematic categories that emerged from the data. Into those categories were placed related themes that fit and they are discussed here. In addition to the four intergenerational-thematic categories, I close this chapter with a discussion of a significant metatheme: collective achievement. This overarching construct arose from the experiences and insights shared in the narrative accounts of my participants.

THEMATIC CATEGORIES

The thematic categories identified in this study offer a road map for understanding African American males' educational experiences in American society. The three families' stories of their educational journeys over 63 years share a common lens through four major categories. Those categories are: safety and masculinity, role models and role of community, resources, and school experiences. A discussion of each category and themes within those categories follows.

Resiliency (Safety and Masculinity)

While many may imagine, and much of the research supports, that a study about African American males school experiences would focus on problematic behaviors on their part, yet my participants' stories revealed that their behaviors were grounded in defensive and offensive stances they employed in response to feeling unsafe in the various contexts they must negotiate in their lives. The theme of safety was a common thread running across the generations. Understandings of and responses to safety were clearly grounded in the participants' experiences as African American males as well as in the experiences of other African American males in their families and communities.

Under the category of Resiliency (Safety and Masculinity), the themes that capture the participants' experiences are the following: lessons learned from older males in family, negative incidents with teachers, the threat of racism, peer buffers vs. peer perpetrators (urban masculinity), and the threat of violence in community.

Lessons Learned From Older Males in Family. The narrative accounts of the participants suggested that fathers play a more significant role in helping their sons navigate the socio-emotional behavioral aspects of school than offering ways to negotiate the academic terrain of school. Nearly all participants mentioned learning from the experiences of the older males, specifically their fathers, to help them deal with personal challenges they experienced in school. These challenges were often centered on their interactions with peers in school. Jeremy Anderson, for example, shared that his father and older brother always gave him advice about "staying out of trouble" and not making decisions to "clown around" or "get into mischief with peers":

> Whenever I talk to my dad about some of the things my friends and I want to do to have fun behind my teachers' backs. He always says, been there, done that—you don't want to do that. And I know when he says that he is serious because he would always get into trouble for playing around when he was my age. I listen. Sometimes I'll tell my brother about a problem I'm having with somebody at school and he asks me questions to get me to think before I do something I'll regret.

His older brother, Shaun, received advice from his father whenever he encountered a problem with someone at school:

> My dad tells me to think about how I treat people and how I would feel if someone did that to me. It makes me think about how I behave with my friends and teachers at school.

According to Tyreek Wallace, his father's advice helped him keep his cool at school and stay away from getting into conflicts with his peers:

> When I stayed behind in fourth grade, there were kids that made fun of me and I was really mad. Very mad about them teasing me, but then I would hear

my dad's voice in my head telling me to ignore them and just stay focused on taking care of my work. It helped, I never hit nobody and they stopped when I didn't fall for the bait.

Tyrone Freeman's dad, Joshua, gave him advice about fighting: "He tells me to think about what will happen if I fight and to use my brain, not my hands, and I'll win." While accounts were told of fathers asking if homework was done, most of the fathers' priorities were on keeping their sons safe in school.

Negative Incidents with Teachers. Nearly all participants in the study talked about the impact of negative incidents with teachers that made indelible impressions on their minds. These encounters left many of them angry and confused about their teachers' perceptions of them. Oftentimes, these negative incidents occurred in the classroom and involved teachers not being fair to them, accusing them of cheating, not keeping private information confidential as promised, making fun of their mistakes in front of classmates, openly accusing them of trying to do more than what was expected, encouraging them to lower their own expectations for themselves as learners, not following through on promises, lying to students' parents, being physically inappropriate (i.e. pushing; or grabbing students), making racist and culturally-insensitive comments to students; and not encouraging or expressed disdain for students' interests. The impact of negative incidents with teachers can be illustrated by two comments by Tyreek Wallace and James Anderson. According to Tyreek:

I just don't trust my teacher, I don't like him because he told my parents that I need to be in special education and he didn't tell me. He acts like I'm doing so well and then when I'm not around he tells them something else. How can he do that? My parents told me what he said. That's just wrong.

The following comment by James spoke to an insensitive teacher he had:

She was just a racist. She treated the Black kids terribly and gave all her energy to the White kids. You could see it in her eyes. I know she hated me—hated us. It didn't matter what I did. She had it in for me. She didn't want to teach me. I worked hard and she didn't care. The two other Black kids in the class suffered in silence. Eventually, I did too.

These comments and others suggest that at an early age, boys have a systematic way in which they identify with and connect to the adults who support them and have a clear sense of those who do not.

Threat of Racism. For many if not all of my participants, the threat of racism manifesting itself was a daily reality both inside and outside of school. On a generational scale, racism and discrimination continued to be a part of their lives as African American males in our society. First is a comment from the oldest participant, Jacob Freeman, who talked about the possibility of prison or even death in the antebellum South:

> Listen, racism was no joke, we had to be very careful around White folks because they hated us and they weren't afraid to hurt us. You didn't give them a reason by being in the wrong place at the wrong time. You could come up dead. The rules were clear it was their world and they didn't want us in it—laws or not.

Moving a few generations forward, after desegregation we find that schools and classrooms may have been integrated, but with integration racism was now both in and outside of the classroom.

According to Charles Anderson and Martin Wallace, going to school during the early years of school desegregation did not change people's perceptions of one another. Charles remembered White students alongside their parents who were picketing outside of his school when Black students were bused into their neighborhood school. Martin commented on the racism at his school at the time:

> The racial tension was thick. Mobs of White kids would come after the Black kids after school. It was hell getting to school in the morning and another hell at the end of the day. It was ridiculous! In class you be sitting next to somebody that wanted to get you once you left the building. Nothing ever happened in the classroom. But it affected people, how do you concentrate on learning anything when you thinking about that.

These older males' stories across the generations revealed their struggles within a racist society.

For the three youngest participants, racism still existed. Unlike their elders, it was now more subtle, more insidious, and closer than ever before. It existed in their classrooms. Ten-year-old Jeremy Anderson discussed how comments made by some of his former teachers had racist undertones: "There are certain things you just don't say like I'm going to 'hang you' to a student, especially a Black one." Additionally, eleven-year-old Tyreek Wallace discussed how racism lived in the low expectations of some of his former teachers: "You can just tell that White teachers treat you differently if you're Black and not in a good way." This comment by eleven-year-old Tyrone Freeman best illustrates these boys' perspective:

> Sometimes I just watch teachers and I can tell which ones don't like Black people. They act real funny and mean. I can tell by what they don't tell us, and what they don't let us do. They racist, but they be trying to hide it. We ain't stupid, we know, we just can't do nothing about it.

Across the generations, racism has existed in and beyond school and it is the responsibility of the child to make sense of it.

Peer Buffers vs. Peer Perpetrators: Urban Masculinities.   Several of the participants discussed the role that peers played around issues of safety in their lives. Peers can and have served as either protective buffers from the threat of violence in school or they can be the perpetrators of teasing, bullying, and physical abuse. The following examples illustrate the two extremes. Tyreek Wallace commented on negative peer interactions:

> Some kids want to act tough and then everybody else ends up acting tough. Nobody really wants to fight, they just scared that if they don't act that way somebody will come after them. It's crazy, people be fighting and calling each other names over stupid stuff. Sometimes I just keep to myself.

For Tyrone Freeman, this state of toughness was somewhat eased by having friends at school and keeping them close for protection:

> There are older kids who just want to start trouble so I have friends who watch out for me and will help me, when people be trying to push me around and stuff. They got my back and I have theirs. We don't really want to fight but we will cause if you don't, they'll just keep bothering you.

Larry Freeman commented on his perceptions of the media's influence on perpetuating hyper-masculine images of African American males. According to him, "These images on television and the radio have gone unchallenged for a long time and they are doing a disservice to young impressionable boys." Issues of masculinity became another aspect of what African American boys must negotiate in schools.

Threat of Violence in Community.   Most of the African American males in this study lived in communities where the threat of violence in their communities was pervasive. The landscape for the urban low-income family is oftentimes one of drugs, violence, police brutality, and crime. Schools located in these areas can play the role of being a safe haven from this reality, but in the case of my participants, they frequently did not. Joshua Freeman commented to this effect:

> Kids don't play outside in the projects because it's just not safe. The stories are true, people will open fire and don't care who's around. It's usually over drugs and money. That's why you hardly ever see little kids outside without an adult.

According to Tyreek Wallace, the threat of violence in the community was very real. He stated:

> Sometimes I'll watch guys from just standing on the corner at night just there waiting to make a deal. These are young guys, too. They just get caught up in the streets and the streets are gonna get them locked up or kill 'em. I don't go outside sometimes 'cause people just be wanting to pull you in stuff or they just want to take your stuff. Some of my friends be telling me that people be rolling up on them in their school trying to get them to sell drugs. It's mad crazy.

It would seem that Black boys are always negotiating the spaces in which they find themselves.

121

Role Models and Role of Community

Across the generations, the participants in this study stated that finding role models in the context of schools was a major challenge. They shared their insights into the dearth of positive African American male role models. These boys and men believed positive role models existed in their homes and communities and questioned why schools and teachers do not tap into them. The themes that fell into this category are: Fathers and Father Figures: Black Role Models Do Exist, Ballers and Rappers, Same Ole Black History Month, Lure of the Streets aka Drugs R' Us, and Is School an Option?

Fathers and Father Figures: Black Role Models Do Exist. For many of the participants, the significance of indirect communication about schooling among African American male family and community members was important. These not-so-subtle messages affect children's understanding of the importance education may, or may not, play in their own lives. The participants believed these were their real-life role models. For the Anderson brothers, Jeremy and Shaun, their father was a major role model in their lives. He also served as a role model for his cousin, James. Larry Freeman definitely saw his father as a role model and one of his "best supporters and toughest critics." Tyreek Wallace saw his father as a viable role model not only for himself and his older cousin, but for many of his friends who did not live with their fathers. He was also aware of many other role models in his community who were successful in their chosen professions. According to Tyreek, "Teachers can be role models for children if they encourage them to do well in school and in life."

This sentiment was echoed by several participants in this study, who believed teachers needed to understand that just because a student may not live with his father, it did not the student lacked father figures in his life. Throughout history, the extended family has had a great influence on the raising and socializing of children. According to Larry Freeman, the seemingly fatherless student will usually have a host of other males involved in his life, whether it is an uncle, a cousin, a brother, or even a neighbor. The roles these males play must be taken into account and seen as resources of support, both socially and academically.

Ballers and Rappers. Four participants made comments about the problematic nature of the two major career options associated with successful African American males: basketball and the rap music industry. Based on my own work in urban schools, I know these were the two choices most frequently shared by young African American males in response to the question: "What do you want to be when you grow up?" The following comments demonstrate the problematic nature of this widely spread phenomenon in urban settings.

First is the youngest of the four participants on this theme, Tyrone Freeman, age 11, who saw doing well in school, at this point in his life, in relation to receiving a scholarship to play college basketball. Then there is Joshua, his stepfather, who saw basketball as a viable way for many urban low-income youth to get out of the environment in which they currently live. On the other hand, Joshua shared how basketball should not be the only option for poor urban youth and that schools need to help them have more options. According to 21-year-old James Anderson:

Teachers and schools automatically just assume that all African American males are only interested in basketball and rap music, and never bother to challenge these perceptions for themselves and for the benefit of their students. Not every Black boy wants this deep down—it's almost like we're being brainwashed to think we should want to be a rapper or a basketball star. That's about making money for somebody else, that ain't about us. Besides most of these kids are not gonna make it and it's not their fault. If we're not showing them something else to aspire to why should they believe they could do anything else and be successful.

Eleven-year-old Tyreek Wallace and James Anderson both believed that the media and the recording industry were responsible for perpetuating these images in the minds of society to the point that African American males buy into the image of what successful African American males must do to be financially successful, even though many of these images run counter to who these boys are and thus create unrealistic expectations and unfulfilled dreams for young African American males. Joshua made the point that "There are many rappers with degrees but they don't ever talk about getting an education because it doesn't fit the image that sells." For Larry Freeman, "Schools are supposed to help children see more options through education, unfortunately many kids don't experience that."

Same Ole Black History Month.   Three participants addressed the lack of culturally responsive curriculum and teaching in their schooling. They claimed that the contributions of African Americans was lacking across subject areas and that African Americans were visibly absent in the books they are required to read in their classes. They believed that this caused African American students to disengage from learning. As James Anderson stated: "The only time we read about Black people was when the textbook had a page or two on slavery and even then it was like it happened a long time ago and now everything is fine." Twenty-three year-old Joshua Freeman said this about his schooling experience:

It's like Black people never did anything except be slaves, play sports, and make music. Which is not true, we made a whole lot of contributions to this country, to the world. It's like they don't want us to know who we really are. It's like this is our history: slavery, Martin Luther King, Malcolm X, Michael Jordan, Jay Z, Oprah, and Tiger Woods. And that's not history those are people who made history. There's a whole lot more than that but White people are really scared of us. The teachers don't know Black history and most them wouldn't know what to do with it. They ain't scared of the people I just said—

two of them ain't alive no more and they love Oprah. Oprah needs to do a show on Blacks in history. Maybe we'll all learn something. Maybe if Barack Obama becomes President he can do something. Make teachers learn history, real history, not just Black history. We are a part of history, period. It's not separate.

Eleven-year-old Tyreek Wallace commented on when the contributions of African Americans were regularly found in schools:

February is Black History Month and that's when we hear about the same four or five people, year after year. It's a waste of time to keep hearing the same speeches, the same books, the same stuff. There's got to be more and why only in February, we're Black all year long. It's just the same ole Black History month every time.

From the 11-year-old to the 23-year-old, these participants made astute observations of the ways in which schools were not culturally responsive to them and the possible impact this can have on the learning for "all" students.

Lure of the Streets aka Drugs R'Us. Many of the participants in this study discussed the role of drugs and the negative images associated with African American males within schools and society. They shared that when people mention drugs, the image coming to mind is usually of a young Black male. James Anderson said, "If you're young and African American in an urban area, then people just automatically assume that you are using or selling drugs, or both." This sentiment was echoed by Joshua Freeman, but he went further: "The pull of the streets is strong on young Black males because there aren't too many options to make money and everybody wants to make big money, fast money." Tyreek Wallace spoke of this option this way: "fast money that way means fast death. It's not like in the movies or the videos. Kids are messing up their lives." Jacob Freeman was the harshest critic of the drug trade and saw drugs in the African American community as "an intentionally placed stumbling block" by Whites to control and further oppress African Americans.

Is School an Option?. This theme flowed consistently through all of the participants' stories. The pervasive question was whether schools as currently structured were really an option for African American males. Many participants believe that African American males have fallen victim to teachers and schools because neither teachers nor schools have been truly invested in their achievement. As James Anderson suggested, "Schools are invested in maintaining the status quo and the status quo has African American males as low achievers. And low achievers don't have any power to change anything." For Martin Wallace, the public school system is simply "not working for us." He added: "We as a people can believe in education all we want, but until the people who are running the schools believe in our education, then it's just an uphill battle for us."

124

Resources

The participants in the study turned a critical eye to what was and remained missing for them in their schools. The information they shared proved to be informative for many reasons. The boys who were currently in school offered a very clear understanding of the impact the lack of resources had on their trust and engagement in the learning process. They also made astute observations about how this lack of resources affected the curriculum and the way they were taught in school. Many believed that for African American males, the system was designed to exclude their interests from the start. Several participants suggested that teachers' negative perceptions of African American males have perpetuated the negative cycle at work in schools, thereby affecting their achievement.

Boredom in School.   Boys learn early to search and rely on male role models who extend outside of the traditional father-son paradigm. In the case of one of youngest participants, Tyreek Wallace pointed out that for himself and many of his peers, their favorite rappers held much allure for them. He stated they often assumed the behaviors and mannerisms of these individuals in school because it helped them cope with being bored and got them attention from their peers. Unfortunately, it also attracted negative attention from their teachers because these behaviors ran counter to behaviors deemed appropriate in school. Another boy in the study described how teachers made students do the same things repeatedly in school. According to 10-year-old Tyrone Freeman:

> We do the same worksheets over and over. It's boring. It's not like schools on TV. Those schools look like fun. They think we don't know what good schools do. We just be bored and that's why kids always getting in trouble. We want to do better stuff than what they give us. If the White kids get it, we should get it.

Children have an understanding of their behavior; they know they are bored, while White teachers only see them as merely misbehaving and hand out worksheets to them.

Lack of Student Engagement.   Student engagement is an important topic in today's urban classrooms. Oftentimes, urban schools are the most under-resourced settings. For all three boys participating in this study, the lack of resources at their schools was cited as a reason for their disengagement. Jeremy Anderson talked about the need for better books and more computers at his school. Tyreek Wallace called attention to the lack of science materials and science curriculum in his former classroom; he also commented on the need for more up-to-date books. Lastly, Tyrone Freeman had the most to say about the lack of resources at his school. He was adamant about the need for "better books," more "hands-on" materials, "instruments for music class," and "more computers." Several of the older males in the study reflected on the lack of access to resources at their schools when they were younger and noted how these materials would have helped them connect to their work in positive and constructive ways.

We Like Science, Too.   While several participants discussed their interest in science, most did not have experiences in school that consistently nurtured this interest in the subject. In describing "a science project" he did at home for school which actually won an award from school, Tyreek Wallace complained that his own classroom teacher offered no support or acknowledgment of his work. Tyrone Freeman talked about why he liked "doing science," but noted how his experiences with science were noticeably tapering off as he moved through school. According to Tyrone, "They be acting like we only like art and gym. You know we like science, too. They should ask us." Some of the older participants, like James Anderson and Joshua Freeman, expressed a love of science despite a lack of encouragement in their schools, while Larry Freeman had had a science teacher in middle school who helped her students appreciate science as much as she did because of her enthusiasm.

School Is Important.   All the participants in this study discussed the importance of school in great depth across the generations. Even for participants who did not perform well academically, there was a strong internal sense that school or education in general was valuable. Many expressed that unfortunately this value, and how it manifested itself in their schooling, was largely dependent on the supports they received from adults both in and outside of school. For these African American males, it was never a question of whether school was important; it was more a question for those running the schools—"Do they believe that school is important for us?"

Outdated Curriculum.   For many of the participants, the curriculum they experienced as African American males was lacking in substance, especially in how it reflected the African American experience. Several of the participants, as suggested by the section above titled "Same Ole Black History Month," explained encountering texts that mentioned slavery and a few key historic figures repeatedly. According to James Anderson, "Teachers need to learn African American history beyond what is presented in textbooks to inspire and motivate their students." He further suggested that White students also need to learn African American history. For Joshua Freeman and Jacob Freeman, this outdated curriculum offers African American students a very skewed view of their community and has little connection to their lives, thereby ultimately impacting the group's self-esteem.

Teachers' Perceptions and Investment.   All the males in this study talked about being able to read their teachers' perceptions of them as students based on how the teachers treated them and their families. They could measure, in their own ways, whether a teacher they had was committed to their social, emotional, and academic well being. Several participants discussed how this was not limited to racial lines because they have encountered teachers of color who seemed to hold negative perceptions of them

as African American males. They also suggested how this became a huge barrier to their success in school. Almost all the adult males discussed how powerful teachers' perceptions and investment were to enhance and maintain student achievement.

School Experiences

For the participants in this study, teachers were major players in their lives. Many cited negative encounters with teachers that seemed to open old wounds. All the males had experienced at least one good teacher in their lives, but one good teacher against a cadre of bad teachers really lowered the odds of outstanding academic achievement for African American boys in today's schools. Under the category of School Experiences, themes capturing the participants' experiences fell into the following categories: Supportive Teachers, Supporting Culturally Responsive Teachers, Questions of Trust, Status Quo Teachers, Impact of Teachers on Image of African American Boys, and Teaching as an Option for African American Males.

Supportive Teachers. Boys have a systematic way in which they identify and connect with the adults who support them and they have a clear sense of those who do not. The three young boys in this study all shared stories of incidents with teachers that let them know whether those teachers truly supported them or not. In their stories, it appeared that unsupportive teachers did not have an understanding of the impact of their actions and never addressed how the boys may have interpreted their actions. According to all the participants, supportive teachers were culturally responsive, caring, smart, engaging, humorous, and loving.

Supporting Culturally Responsive Teachers. Two participants remembered specific teachers who were invested in understanding and embracing the cultural backgrounds of their students. As a result, these teachers were popular teachers among the students and their families. Unfortunately, these teachers were often not well received and supported by their colleagues at school. Joshua Freeman talked about one teacher he had in high school who left the school because, according to him, "other teachers did not like this teacher 'cause the teacher looked out for us." Tensions among the faculty about how some teachers "work well" with students of color made invested teachers the targets of their colleagues. Joshua suggested that the school system needed to be more embracing of teachers "who look out for us" and use them as models for other teachers to emulate.

Questions of Trust. Many participants highlighted issues of trust with the adults in their schools. For example, Tyrone Freeman shared how he has lost trust with his school counselor after she shared confidential information with other adults at his school. For James Anderson, a trusting relationship with one teacher in high school helped him cope with his mistrust of the advice he got from another teacher who was not supporting his academic growth. For all of the males in this study, having an adult in their lives whom they trusted helped them cope with issues both in school and within their communities.

Status Quo Teachers. In describing both past and present teachers they had, the study participants revealed that some of these individuals made an investment in maintaining the status quo. The status quo keeps African American males from succeeding in school and the participants shared stories of teachers who seemed to be invested in maintaining this status quo. James Anderson shared how one teacher's low expectations for him colored her interactions with him and his schoolwork. For Jacob Freeman, these low expectations were a constant reality that African Americans from the South had to contend with, especially with White teachers that their children had in the North. Joshua Freeman talked about teachers who just did not seem to want to see their students do any better in school and had no investment in seeing things differently.

Power of Teachers and Teaching. All the participants discussed the power that teachers have in changing the negative images of African American males that exist in school and society through their work in the classrooms. Three participants in particular commented on the responsibility of teachers in countering these existing negative images. Martin Wallace commented on how teachers were image-makers, along with parents, for African American males. James Anderson discussed how teachers must understand that a few supportive actions and words on their part can have a tremendous impact on a child's future. Jacob Freeman noted how male teachers can and should embrace the responsibility of being positive father figures for their students. His stance was that "classrooms need to be more like family" if we are going to change things for the better.

Several participants mentioned their interest in teaching as a future career. Shaun Anderson was seriously considering being a teacher and cited his father as his inspiration. Larry Freeman spent time in the classroom as a teaching assistant and tutor, and expressed a desire to give back to the community, possibly via teaching in the future. Joshua Freeman, despite his academic shortcomings to date, also expressed an enthusiastic interest in teaching and felt that his own experiences will help him connect with his potential future students. Ironically, the youngest participant, Tyrone Freeman, claimed he did not want to consider teaching because he did not want to be like the negative teachers he has experienced in his own schooling. Thus far, James Anderson definitely wanted to teach in the future and had strong ideas around educational reform to bring change for African American males and all students.

METATHEME: COLLECTIVE ACHIEVEMENT

All of these themes, emerging from the data, have shed light on an overarching metatheme that runs across the generations and ties these participants' schooling experiences together. This thus suggests what could bring change, not only to educational outcomes for African American males, but also to the schools and communities serving them. My analysis uncovered the metatheme of collective achievement.

Collective Achievement in Context: Past, Present, and Future

Collective achievement encapsulates all of the suggestions and possibilities that constituted the schooling experiences of African American males participating in this study. I returned to the literature and discovered that collective achievement was not a new term or phrase. In a study conducted in the 1960s of students in historically Black colleges, Patricia Gurin and Edgar Epps (1975) used the term collective achievement to discuss issues of Black consciousness, identity, and achievement in the lives of their participants. The researchers focused on achievement as a collective phenomenon:

> It focuses on the collective commitments and action of the students through which they tried to exact legal, economic, and social changes that would benefit Black people. The activists were striving to achieve, but they were working for group products and accomplishments rather than for individual goals. Their motivation carried all the usual connotations of achievement motivation: it prompted hard and persistent effort as well as setting group goals that were both difficult and realistic. When successful in creating change, they evinced the kind of pleasure usually related to achievement. They were elated with a job well done; they were proud of the process of working together. (p. 189)

The current study expanded on this term by extending its application to the work of multiple groups or stakeholders around the issue of student achievement.

In today's educational context of the Achievement Gap and Disproportionality in Special Education, as well as the so-called crisis with Black males, there is much debate about the engagement and achievement of African American boys in school. A significant body of research is supported by quantitative measures such as low test scores, high dropout rates, crime and incarceration statistics, suggesting that African American males are not successful in school or in society. Even in the era of the No Child Left Behind Act and the systemic educational reforms it has ushered into our schools, African American males continue to occupy the bottom tiers in terms of achievement.

The challenge of addressing the current state of affairs is great and will require a level of engagement, investment, and achievement for all who play a role and have a stake in bringing change for African American males. Where educational policy and research have primarily focused their lens solely on the achievement and outcomes of African American boys at all levels of school, there seems to be a void that fails to capture the achievement of all stakeholders involved in children's academic success and life outcomes. We are in desperate need of a lens that taps into the achievement of not just our students, but also their families, their teachers, school administration, school staff, and the community. A new vision of collective achievement would not only provide a constructive way of looking at and understanding student achievement, but would provide important applications for investment and engagement as well.

Defining and Framing Collective Achievement

As I reflected on my own history in schools as both student and teacher—in the roles of a professional development specialist, an educational researcher, a teacher educator, a collaborator with multiple stakeholders, and now a researcher—the concept of collective achievement encapsulates all of what we in education continue to grapple with regarding African American males. I believe that the lens of collective achievement forces us to go even more deeply than the *what* of engagement and investment into the *who* as it relates to achievement, and not just for the students but for everyone involved in the educational process. My work as a teacher has allowed me to see how this lens can be applied to everyone's continued engagement and achievement. Schools need to identify and put into operation a collective achievement framework, which capitalizes on and honors the engagement and investments of all stakeholders.

Making Meaning Around Collective Achievement

The narrative stories of the African American males participating in this study across the generations revealed a common thread about education. It is multifaceted and it involves the work of many—students, parents, community members, administrators, and others. The analysis of these narratives revealed that, simply put, good schooling is invested in collective achievement and bad schooling is not invested in collective achievement

Most of the males in the study have experienced more of the later. They were also clearly able to, regardless of age, articulate and extrapolate what teaching that is invested in collective achievement should look like. It is caring, filled with high expectations, it is resourceful, it is culturally responsive, it is dynamic, it is connected and builds on other stakeholder contributions, and it does not matter who is doing it—male, female, Black, White, or any other possibility. Most importantly, according to the youngest participants in this study: it should be fun.

QUESTIONS TO CONSIDER

When questions such as these are considered through the lens of collective achievement, responses may be different:

– Where in the curriculum of teacher education does collective achievement exist?
– Where does collective achievement exist in each component of the school curriculum?
– How does collective achievement exist in schools, at home, and in the community?
– Where does collective achievement exist in school reform efforts?
– In what ways is collective achievement a part of accountability?

Ladson Billing's (1994, 1995) work on culturally responsive curriculum and pedagogy provided a framework for reforming teacher education and impacting student achievement for marginalized students. Collective achievement builds on her seminal work and offers another framework that will reach not only students and teachers, but all stakeholders in and outside the classroom.

The question we must ask ourselves is: should students' academic trajectory be predetermined by the assumptions and beliefs that teachers have of students, their families, and their communities? No, but it happens every day in schools, based on teachers' perceptions of the educational legacy—the educational experiences that are passed on generation to generation—that enters the classroom with each student they teach. The demographics of the majority who are teaching in public school classrooms today are White, middle-class females, in contrast to the students they teach, who are mostly students of color. Again, what assumptions do teachers make because of differences in race, ethnicity, gender, and class? How do teachers view and respond to the educational legacies that walk into schools and classrooms each day? These are critical questions that teachers and schools must ask.

I was an elementary school teacher in a large urban public school system for several years prior to pursuing my doctoral studies. A few years ago, I attended the eighth grade graduation ceremony of my former third grade students. After the ceremony, I found myself locked in a warm embrace with a former student and his family. As we shared in this moment of celebration, this African American mother said to me, "You did it, you should be so proud. Look at what you've done, all your hard work." Still hugging them, I said, "No, look at what *we've* done." Now, through the lens of this research study, I see that moment as a defining moment of collective achievement. In lifting each of their roles, I then addressed my own. I told the graduate's mother that she got him ready for school every day and attended conferences. I reminded the father that he read books with him on the bus to and from school. I shared with his aunt how she helped him with his homework after school. And to the student, I said, "You worked hard and wanted to learn." I was able to do my work because from the start, I acknowledged and incorporated their work into my own. On that graduation day, I shared in many moments such as this that I now see are key examples of collective achievement. These moments continue to resonate in my head and have helped me put the pieces together, in concert with the literature, and most definitely with the voices of the African American males in this study. The final Chapter IX next presents conclusions and implications for practice as well as future research that have stemmed from these insights.

COLLECTIVE ACHIEVEMENT AND TRUE SCHOOL REFORM

WHAT HAVE WE LEARNED FROM AFRICAN AMERICAN MALES?

The African American males who participated in this study were a diverse group of individuals with similar and different educational experiences. A recognized strength of qualitative research is that it allows for in-depth focus on a small number of participants, unlike quantitative studies that cover breadth involving many people in large samples. This small-scale sample of three families, with 11 participants in total, may not necessarily be applicable to the schooling experiences of all African American males across generations. What these narratives do, however, is demonstrate the complexity involved in how African American males view and discuss their schooling experiences and how these stories are connected across generations.

Osborne's (1997) perspective on African American male academic success being directly attributed to whether students identify with academics has been deepened by the current findings. The participants in this study revealed that they did indeed identify with academics. Yet, they questioned whether the academic environment of schools and teachers identified with them. This perspective shifted the sole ownership of academic success and achievement from the students, suggesting a multiple stakeholder gap in the achievement of African American male students. Regarding Steele's (1992) stereotype threat model, which suggests negative stereotypes hinder the academic performance of African American males, the findings from the current study also support his work.

Ogbu's (1997) cultural ecological perspective, which suggests that the home culture and community with which students identify will impact their school performance, scratches the surface of the dynamics at work in urban communities. The current study looked more in-depth at those dynamics across generations and found that the participants did come from home cultures that placed value on education, although the home value was not enough to combat what they met in school. The challenges that the students and their families faced while operationalizing this belief in school have not usually been taken into account by researchers in their attempts to explain the Achievement Gap. The responses of the participants in this study were in keeping with Ogbu's perspective that schools are sometimes a continuation of societal oppression. In the present study, 73-year-old Jacob Freeman expressed this sentiment well:

> For African American males schools try to get you ready for society. But society don't want you there. So the bad schools are getting you ready for a bad place, a bad position in society. That's how they see you. So many schools are just not trying to educate our kids for a better future. It's just more of the same thing.

His comment was based on years of life experience and watching how the generations after his fare in society today.

The findings also supported Majors and Billson's (1992) cool-pose theory, which purports that African American males adopt a "cool" stance in school as a coping mechanism. The findings further suggested that this stance is also connected to mirroring media images of themselves they encounter, which are peer-motivated and connected to peer dynamics that adults do not fully understand.

Moreover, the current findings also supported Noguera's (2003a) environmental and cultural perspective, which suggests that the interaction of harmful environmental and cultural factors have an impact on young African American males in and outside of school. The current study expanded on this by suggesting that these harmful factors should not be viewed as being isolated to the African American community; on the contrary, some of these harmful factors are originating in the schools themselves and do not help African American males positively negotiate these different contexts.

In addition, notions of the nuclear family simply do not convey the wondrous array of family groupings that have always existed in the African American community. This is directly related to the existence of unrecognized role models that exist in the African American community.

WHAT CAN WE DO?

In examining the schooling experiences and achievement of African American males, educators and researchers have not often viewed them as being knowledgeable informants of their own experiences. Contrary to this approach, I asked African American boys and men to share their schooling experiences with me and they did. My participants taught me about how they negotiated their identity as African American males and navigated the terrain of availability and access to opportunity regarding their education. These are voices of experience that can inform the work of educators, administrators, researchers, parents, community organizations, and policymakers. Collective achievement is a model of reciprocity. The fates of teachers and students are linked, and breed shared responsibility and shared accountability.

IMPLICATIONS FOR PRACTICE

African American families value education. Their engagement and investment in the schooling process of their children has often been interpreted in ways that point out their limitations instead of the limitations of the public school system in this society. The implications for practice are overwhelmingly clear. The findings from this study have significant implications for school reform. The adoption and implementation of collective achievement frameworks are of the utmost importance in changing educational outcomes for African American males. The findings suggested that culturally responsive professional development must be mandated for teachers and administrators. Teacher education programs must provide prospective teachers with culturally responsive pedagogy and teach them history through multiple perspectives. The findings also suggested that outdated and culturally exclusionary curriculum must become a thing of the past to truly engage and positively impact teacher investment and student achievement. Schools need to build stronger relationships within the communities they serve and find the various human resources that exist, and in collaboration with them redefine collective achievement.

IMPLICATIONS FOR FUTURE RESEARCH

Understanding the schooling experiences of African American males from their perspective has much to contribute to the field of education. The collective voice of African American males is missing from the research literature in two significant areas, both on an intergenerational and an elementary school level. The findings from the current study call for additional research that explores the schooling experiences of African American boys to better understand how they experience the captive environments of classrooms and schools.

There is also a need for research that captures and examines the experiences of multiple stakeholders in young African American boys' schooling. Such research could help identify and understand the continuities and discontinuities at work in the education of African American males.

Existing research has relied heavily on quantitative measures to tell the educational experiences of African American males. This approach leaves many aspects of African American males' schooling experiences unexamined and leaves many avenues for reform unidentified and unexplored. While quantitative data have given us numerical information about how African American males are doing in and beyond school, qualitative data will give deeper meaning to existing data and help us understand why schools are not working for African American males. Research that is truly invested in the academic achievement of African American males must use qualitative measures to inform, explain, and challenge the quantitative measures and their value in defining the schooling experiences of African American males. If 10-year-olds are so articulate about their experiences in school, what would even younger boys' stories reveal?

EPILOGUE

The stories of the 11 African American males in this study presented the complexities of the intersection of race, gender, and class in the lives of the three families. The stories revealed how for African American males, the images and perceptions that exist within American society have a far-reaching influence on the ways African American males are treated by others and, more importantly, how they treat themselves. The cross-generational stories of the men and boys within these families overlapped and intersected in a complex tapestry that demonstrates how the African American male experience of education continues to transcend the boundaries of time, space, and place. The starting point for African American males began when the first slave ships arrived in America. It is a story replete with pain, hardship, and even death in pursuit of education. It is a story of broken families, concrete-over-glass ceilings, and unrealized dreams. It is also one of astonishing hope and resiliency in the face of a society that is haunted by the ghosts of its past and overshadowed by present racism and discrimination.

The public education system in the United States, in under-serving generation after generation of African American males, has deprived itself and society of the innate gifts and talents that continue to go malnourished in classrooms today. It is a system whose tests and evaluations have been used to paint the bleakest picture of failure for African American males, who continue to be the voiceless group in education. The system has often misspoken for and misrepresented them as being deficient, unengaged, and lacking motivation. Clearly, in talking to this small group of African American males in this study, the system has made an error in judgment. Who better to reflect back on the education system's intergenerational shortcomings and be the best informants of long overdue educational reform than the group who continues to be at the bottom looking up—and sometimes down—and on the outside looking in and turning away.

There are those in society who argue that the past is the past and slavery has ended. They also argue that African American males do not take full advantage of the open opportunities that exist in education and, therefore, society. Those who make these arguments are in denial that racism does not continue to modernize along with everything else in this society. While its nature is still systemic, it has taken on the subtlest hues and textures in our daily lives today. Again, those who would argue against this by citing examples of African Americans occupying, or potentially occupying, positions in society for the first time as a symbol that change has come are missing the point of where change must occur: in the actions and minds of those historically privileged in America. They must see the linkages between their success and achievement, and the lack of similar outcomes for those who have not had the same access to resources they have had. Yes, it is in the actions and minds of those who have occupied these very same positions of power for generation after generation to which a handful of African Americans are only now gaining access. We are still living in an era where successful African Americans must oftentimes be proclaimed as "the first Black (insert title here)." It is an error on the part of those who have not taken responsibility for engaging and investing in the future educational and societal success of African American males. I argue that change will not come if *their* success is not truly seen as *our* success—which ultimately means their failure is our failure.

Collective achievement is a model of reciprocity. Teachers and students are linked in shared responsibility and shared accountability. The questions are: Is our education system ready to be the model for society that it claims to be? Is it ready to transform the lives of African American males and transform its own unquestioned legacy of failure? Are African American males ready to take their rightful place as openly recognized and honored members in this society? In the future, iron bars and barbed wire will not be able to contain the loss of a group that has contributed to this society since its inception, a group that can and will, if supported, lift our society in ways yet to be imagined.

BIBLIOGRAPHY

Allen, R. L., & Bagozzi, R. P. (2001). Cohort differences in the structure and outcomes of an African American belief system. *Journal of Black Psychology, 27*(4), 367–400.

Anyon, J. (1997). *Ghetto schooling: A political economy of urban educational reform*. New York, NY: Teachers College Press.

Aud, S., Fox, M., & KewelRamani, A. (2010. *Status and trends in the education of racial and ethnic groups* (NCES 2010-015). Washington, DC: U.S. Department of Education, National Center for Education Statistics, U.S. Government Printing Office.

Baldwin, J. (1985). *Go tell it on the mountain* (Reissue edition). New York, NY: Laurel.

Benedict, R. (1934). *Patterns of culture*. Boston, MA: Houghton Mifflin Company.

Boas, F. (1982). *Race, language and culture*. Chicago, IL: University of Chicago Press.

Bogdan, R. C., & Biklen, S. K. (2003). *Qualitative research for education: An introduction to theory and methods* (4th ed.). New York, NY: Pearson Education.

Bowman, P. J. & Gadsen, V. (1999). African American males and the struggle toward responsible fatherhood. In V. C. Polite & J. E. Davis (eds.), *African American males in school and society*. New York, NY: Teachers College Press.

Brown v. Board of Education of Topeka, 347 U.S. 483, 74 S. Ct. 686, 98 L. Ed. 873 (1954).

Canada, G. (1998). *Reaching up for manhood: Transforming the lives of boys in America*. Boston, MA: Beacon Press.

Carothers, S. (1990). Catching sense: Learning to be Black and female from our mothers. In F. Ginsberg & A. Lowenhaupt-Tsing (Eds.), *Uncertain terms: Negotiating gender in American culture* (pp. 232–247). Boston, MA: Beacon Press.

Clayton, O., Mincy, R. B., & Blankenhorn, D. (Eds.). (2003). *Black fathers in contemporary American society: Strengths, weaknesses, and strategies for change*. New York, NY: Russell Sage Foundation.

Coles, R. L. (2002). Black single fathers: Choosing to parent full-time. *Journal of Contemporary Ethnography, 31*(4), 411–439.

Cosby, B. (1986). *Fatherhood*. New York, NY: Doubleday.

Cross, W. E., Jr. (1991). *Shades of Black: Diversity in African American identity*. Philadelphia, PA: Temple University Press.

Dance, J. (2002). *Tough fronts: The impact of street culture on schooling*. New York, NY: Routledge Falmer.

Daniel, J. L., & Effinger, M. J. (1996). Bosom biscuits: A study of African American intergenerational communication. *Journal of Black Studies, 27*(2), 183–200.

Datcher, M. (2001). *Raising fences: A Black man's love story*. New York, NY: Riverhead Books.

Davis, J. E. (2003). Early schooling and academic achievement of African American males. *Urban Education, 38*(5), 515–537.

Delpit, L. (1995). *Other people's children: Cultural conflict in the classroom*. New York, NY: The New Press.

Denzin, N. K., & Lincoln, Y. S. (Eds.). (2000). *Handbook of qualitative research*. Thousand Oaks, CA: Sage.

Donnor, J. K., & Schockley, K. G. (2010). Leaving us behind: An interpretation of NCLB and the miseducation of African American males. *Educational Foundations, 24*(3/4), 43–54.

Draughn, P. S., & Waggenstock, M. L. (1986). Fathers' supportiveness: Perceptions of fathers and college daughters. In R. A. Lewis & R. E. Salt (Eds.), *Men in families*. Beverly Hills, CA: Sage.

DuBois, W. E. B. (1973). *The education of Black people*. New York, NY: Monthly Review Press.

Duncan, G. J., & Magnuson, K. (2005). Can family socio-economic resources account for racial and ethnic test score gaps? *Future of Children, 15*, 35–54.

Dundes, A. (1968). Every man his way: Readings in cultural anthropology. In M. Mead (Ed.), *The application of anthropological techniques to cross-national communication*. Englewood Cliffs, NJ: Prentice-Hall.

Ellison, R. (1995). *Invisible man* (2nd ed.). New York, NY: Random House.

Ely, M., Anzul, M., Friedman, T., Garner, D., & Steinmetz, A. M. (1991). *Doing qualitative research: Circles within circles*. New York, NY: Routledge Falmer.

Ely, M., Vinz, R., Downing, M., & Anzul, M. (1997). *On writing qualitative research: Living by words*. Washington, DC: The Falmer Press.

Eyerman, R. (2004). The past in the present: Culture and the transmission of memory. *Acta Sociological, 47*(2), 159–169.

Ferguson, A. A. (2001). *Bad boys: Public schools in the making of black masculinity*. Ann Arbor, MI: University of Michigan Press.

Frazier, E. F. (1966). *The Negro family in the United States*. Chicago, IL: University of Chicago Press.

Fryer, R. G., & Levitt, S. D. (2006). The Black-White test score gap through third grade. *American Law and Economics Review, 8*(2), 249–281.

Gay, G. (2000). *Culturally responsive teaching*. New York, NY: Teachers College Press.

Geertz, C. (1973). Thick description: Toward an interpretive study of culture. In *The interpretation of cultures*. New York, NY: Basic Books.

Gibbs, J. T. (1988). *Young, Black, and male in America*. New York, NY: Auburn House.

Glaser, B. G., & Strauss, A. L. (1967). *The discovery of grounded theory*. Chicago, IL: Aldine.

Gurin, P., & Epps, E. (1975). *Black consciousness, identity, and achievement: A study of students in historically Black colleges*. New York, NY: John Wiley & Sons.

Hale, J. E. (1982). *Black children: Their roots, culture, and learning styles*. Baltimore, MD: Johns Hopkins University Press.

Hale, J. E. (1994). *Unbank the fire: Visions for the education of African American children*. Baltimore, MD: Johns Hopkins University Press.

Haley, A. (1976). *Roots*. New York, NY: Doubleday.

Hamer, J. (2001). *What it means to be daddy: Fatherhood for Black men living away from their children*. New York, NY: Columbia University Press.

Harris, W. G. (1999). Conceptions of the male familial role by African American youth revisted. In W. G. Harris & G. M. Duhon (Eds.), *The African-American male perspective of barriers to success*. New York, NY: Edwin Mellen Press.

Heckathorn, D. D. (1997). Respondent-driven sampling: A new approach to the study of hidden populations. *Social Problems, 44*, 174–199.

Hill, R. B. (2003). *The strengths of Black families*. Lanham, MD: University Press.

Hoffman, K., Llagas, C., & Snyder, T. D. (2003). *Status and trends in the education of Blacks*. Washington, DC: U. S. Department of Education, National Center for Educational Statistics.

Holstein, J. A., & Gubrium, J. F. (1995). *The active interview*. Thousand Oaks, CA: Sage.

hooks, b. (2004). *We real cool: Black men and masculinity*. New York, NY: Routledge.

Hopkins, R. (1997). *Educating Black males: Critical lessons in schooling, community, and power*. Albany, NY: State University of New York Press.

Howard, T. C. (2002). Hearing footsteps in the dark: African American students' descriptions of effective teachers. *Journal of Education for Students Placed At Risk, 7*, 425–444.

Howard, T. C. (2008). Who really cares? The disenfranchisement of African American males in PreK-12 schools: A critical race theory perspective. *Teachers College Record, 110*(5), 954–985.

Hucks, D. C. (2008). *New visions of collective achievement: The cross-generational schooling experiences of African American males*. (Doctoral dissertation). Available from ProQuest Dissertations and Theses database (UMI No. 3332512).

Hughes, R., & Bonner, F. A., II. (2006). Leaving Black males behind: Debunking the myths of meritocratic education. *Journal of Race and Policy, 2*(1), 76–87.

Hughes, D., & Johnson, D. (2001). Correlates in children's experiences of parents' racial socialization behaviors. *Journal of Marriage and Family, 63*(3), 981–995.

Hutchinson, J. F. (1997). *Cultural portrayals of African Americans: Creating and ethnic/racial identity*. Westport, CT: Bergin & Garvey.

Jackson, J. F. L., & Moore, J. L., III (2006). African American males in education: Endangered or ignored? *Teachers College Record, 108*(2), 201–205.

Kohn, A. (1999). *The schools our children deserve: Moving beyond traditional classrooms and "tougher standards."* New York, NY: Houghton Mifflin.

Kotlowitz, A. (1991). *There are no children here: The story of two boys growing up in the other America.* New York, NY: Random House.

Kozol, J. (2005). *The shame of the nation: The restoration of apartheid schooling in America.* New York, NY: Crown.

Kunjufu, J. (1995). *Countering the conspiracy to destroy Black boys.* Chicago, IL: African American Images.

Ladson-Billings, G. (1994). *The dreamkeepers: Successful teaching of African American children.* San Francisco, CA: Jossey-Bass.

Ladson-Billings, G. (1995). Toward a theory of culturally relevant pedagogy. *American Educational Research Journal, 32,* 465–491.

Lareau, A. (2002). Invisible inequality: Social class and childrearing in Black families and White families. *American Sociological Review, 67*(5), 747–776.

Lareau, A., & Horvat, E. M. (1999). Moments of social inclusion and exclusion: Race, class, and cultural capital in family-school relationships. *Sociology of Education, 72*(1), 37–53.

Laubasher, L. (2005). Toward a (de)constructive psychology of African American men. *Journal of Black Psychology, 31*(2), 111–129.

Lawrence-Lightfoot, S. (2003). *The essential conversation: What parents and teachers can learn from each other.* New York, NY: Random House.

Lawrence-Lightfoot, S., & Hoffman, D. J. (1997). *The art and science of portraiture.* San Francisco, CA: Jossey-Bass.

Lawler, S. (2002). Narrative in social research. In T. May (Ed.), *Qualitative research in education* (pp. 242–258). Thousand Oaks, CA: Sage.

Lewis, A. (1966). *The second American revolution: A first-hand account of the struggle for civil rights.* London, UK: Faber.

Lewis, C. W., & Moore, J. L., III. (2008). African American students in K-12 urban educational settings. *Urban Education, 43*(2), 123–126. Doi:10.1177/ 00420859083141147

Lincoln, Y., & Guba, E. (1985). *Naturalistic inquiry.* Newbury Park, CA: Sage.

Lincoln, Y. S., & Guba, E. G. (1989). *Fourth generation evaluation.* Newbury Park, CA: Sage.

Lofland, J., & Lofland, L. H. (1995). *Analyzing social setting: A guide to qualitative observation and analysis* (3rd ed.). New York, NY: Wadsworth.

Majors, R., & Billson, J. (1992). *Cool pose: The dilemma of Black manhood in America.* New York, NY: Lexington Books.

McBride, J. (1996). *The color of water: A Black man's tribute to his White mother.* New York, NY: Riverhead Books.

McDonald, J. (1996). *Redesigning school: Lessons for the 21st century.* San Francisco, CA: Jossey-Bass.

Meier, D. (2002). *In schools we trust: Creating communities of learning in an era of testing and standardization.* Boston, MA: Beacon Press.

Mincy, R. (2006). *Black males left behind.* Washington, DC: Urban Institute Press.

Mincy, R. B. (Ed.). (1994). *Nurturing young Black males: Challenges to agencies, programs, and social policy.* Washington, DC: Urban Institute Press.

Mishler, E. G. (1991). Representing discourse: The rhetoric of transcription. *Journal of Narrative and Life History, 1*) 255–280.

Moore, J. L., III. (2006). A qualitative investigation of African American males' career trajectory in engineering: Implications for teachers, school counselors, and parents. *Teachers College Record, 108*(2), 246–266.

Morrison, T. (1977). *Song of Solomon.* New York, NY: Alfred A. Knopf.

Moynihan, D. P. (1965, Fall). Employment, income and the ordeal of the Negro family. *Daedalus,* 745–69.

National Center for Education Statistics. (2007). *National assessment of educational progress: The nation's report card 2007.* Retrieved from http://www.nces.ed.gov/nationsreportcard

National Urban League. (2008). *The state of Black America 2007: Portrait of the Black male.* New York, NY: Author.

Neblett, E. W., Chavous, T. M., Nguyên, H. X., & Sellers, R. M. (2009, Summer). Say it loud—"I'm Black and I'm proud": Parents' messages about race, racial discrimination, and academic achievement in African American boys. *Journal of Negro Education, 78*(3), 246–262.

No Child Left Behind Act of 2001, 20 U.S.C. § 6319 (2008).

Noguera, P. A. (1996). Responding to the crisis confronting California's Black male youth: Providing support without furthering marginalization. *The Journal of Negro Education, 65,* 219–236.

Noguera, P. (2003a). *City schools and the American dream: Reclaiming the promise of public education.* New York, NY: Teachers College Press.

Noguera, P. A. (2003b). The trouble with Black boys: The role and influence of environmental and cultural factors on the academic performance of African American males. *Urban Education, 38*(4), 431–459.

Noguera, P. A. (2008). *The trouble with Black boys... and other reflections on race, equity and the future of public education.* San Francisco, CA: Jossey-Bass.

Ogbu, J. U. (1974). *The next generation.* New York, NY: Academic Press.

Ogbu, J. U. (1997). Understanding the school performance of urban African Americans: Some essential background knowledge. In H. Walberg, O. Reyes, & R. Weissberg (Eds.), *Children and youth: Interdisciplinary perspectives* (pp. 190–222). London, UK: Sage.

Ogbu, J. U. (2003). *Black American students in an affluent suburb: A study of academic disengagement (Sociocultural, Political, and Historical Studies in Education).* Englewood Cliffs, NJ: Lawrence Erlbaum.

Osborne, J. W. (1997). Race and academic disidentification. *Journal of Educational Psychology, 89,* 728–735.

Osborne, J. W. (1999). Unraveling underachievement among African American boys from an identification with academics perspective. *The Journal of Negro Education, 68*(4), 555–565.

Perry, T., Steele, C., & Hilliard, A., III. (2003). *Young, gifted, and Black: Promoting high achievement among African-American students.* Boston, MA: Beacon Press.

Pluviose, D. (2008 May). Remedying the Black male "crisis." *Diverse Issues in Higher Education, 25*(6), 5.

Polite, V. C. (1999). A cup runneth over: Personal reflections on the Black male experience. In V. C. Polie & J. Davis (Eds.), *African American males in school and society: Practices and policies for effective education.* New York, NY: Teachers College Press.

Polite, V. C., & Davis, J. (Eds.). (1999). *African American males in school and society: Practices and policies for effective education.* New York, NY: Teachers College Press.

Price, J. (1999). Schooling and racialized masculinities: The diploma, teachers, and peers in the lives of young, African American men. *Youth and Society, 31*(2), 224–263.

Rist, R. C. (1970). Student social class and teacher expectations: The self-fulfilling prophecy in ghetto education. *Harvard Educational Review, 40*(3), 441–451.

Rist, R. C. (1973). *The urban school: A factory for failure, a study of education in American society.* Cambridge, MA: MIT Press.

Rowley, L. L., & Bowman, P. J. (2009). Risk, protection, and achievement disparities among African American males: Cross-generation theory, research, and comprehensive intervention. *The Journal of Negro Education, 78,* 305–320.

Rubin, H., & Rubin, I. (1995). *Qualitative interviewing: The art of hearing data.* Thousand Oaks, CA: Sage.

Sampson, W. A. (2002). *Black student achievement: How much do family and school really matter?* Lanham, MD: Scarecrow Press.

Scanzoni, J. H. (1971). *The Black family in modern society.* Boston, MA: Allyn & Bacon.

Schott Foundation for Public Education. (2008). Given half a chance: The Schott 50-state report on public education and black males. Retrieved from www.blackboysreport.org.

Scott, J. W. (1997). Making a way out of no way. In C. Johnson & J. McCluskey, Jr. (Eds.), *Black men speaking.* Bloomington, IN: Indiana University Press.

Sealey-Ruiz, Y. (2007). Rising above reality: The voices of reentry Black mothers and their daughters. *The Journal of Negro Education, 76,* 141–152.

Seidman, I. (1998). *Interviewing as qualitative research: A guide for education and the social sciences* (2nd ed.). New York, NY: Teachers College Press.

Sewell, T. (2000). *Black masculinities and schooling: How black boys survive modern schooling*. London, UK: Trentham Books.

Sleeter, C. (2001). *Culture, difference and power*. New York, NY: Teachers College Press.

Smith, M. W., & Wilhelm, J. D. (2002). *"Reading don't fix no Chevys": Literacy in the lives of young men*. Portsmouth, NH: Heineman.

Stack, C. B. (1997). *All our kin: Strategies for survival in a Black community*. New York, NY: Basic Books.

Steele, C. (1992). Race and schooling of African Americans. *Atlantic Monthly, 4*, 68–78.

Steele, C. (1997). A threat in the air: How stereotypes shape intellectual identity and performance. *American Psychologist, 52*, 613–629.

Steele, S. (1990). *The content of our character: A new vision of race in America*. New York, NY: Harper Collins.

Steele, S. (1998). *A dream deferred: The second betrayal of Black freedom in America*. New York, NY: Harper Collins.

Stevenson, H. C. (2004). Boys in men's clothing. In N. Way & J. Chiu (Eds.), *Adolescent boys*. New York, NY: University Press.

Straus, A. L. (1970). Discovering new theory from previous theory. In T. Shibutani (Ed.), *Human nature and collective behavior: Papers in honor of Herbert Blumer*. Englewood Cliffs, NJ: Prentice-Hall.

Swanson, D. P., Cunningham, M., & Spencer, M. B. (2003). Black males' structural conditions, achievement patterns, normative needs, and opportunities. *Urban Education, 38*, 608–633.

Tate, W. (1994). From inner to ivory tower: Does my voice matter in the academy? *Urban Education, 29*, 245–269.

Tesch, R. (1990). *Qualitative research: Analysis types and software tools*. London: The Falmer Press.

Thompson, G. (2002). *African American teens discuss their schooling experiences*. Westport, CT: Bergin & Garvey.

Thompson, G. (2003). *What African American parents want educators to know*. Westport, CT: Praeger.

Thompson, G. (2004). *Through ebony eyes: What teachers need to know but are afraid to ask about African American students*. San Francisco, CA: Jossey-Bass.

Toldson, I. A. (2008). *Breaking barriers: Plotting the path to academic success for school-aged African-American males*. Washington, DC: Congressional Black Caucus Foundation.

Tunnell, K. D. (1998). Interviewing the incarcerated: Personal notes on ethical and methodological issues. In K. B. deMarrais (Ed.), *Inside stories*. Englewood Cliffs, NJ: Lawrence Erlbaum.

U. S. Bureau of Justice Statistics. (2000). Correctional populations in the United States, 2001. Washington, DC: U.S. Department of Justice. Retrieved from www.ojp.usdoj.gov/bjs/

U. S. Census Bureau (2003). School enrollment data, Census 2000. Washington, DC: U. S. Department of Commerce, Economics, and Statistical Administration. Retrieved from www.census.gov/

Wade, J. C. (1996). African American men's gender role conflict: The significance of racial identity. *Sex Roles, 34*(1/2), 17–33.

Walker, A. (2003). *The color purple*. New York, NY: Harvest Books.

Watson, J. (2006, August). Scholars and activists debate the 'crisis of young Black males.' *Diverse Issues in Higher Education, 23*(13), 8–9.

Weiss, C. (1997). *Evaluation* (2nd ed.). Upper Saddle River, NJ: Prentice-Hall.

Weiss, R. (1995). *Learning from strangers: The art and method of qualitative interview studies*. New York, NY: Free Press.

Wideman, J. E. (1994). *Fatheralong: A meditation on fathers and sons, race and society*. New York, NY: Pantheon.

Willie, C. V., & Reddick, R. J. (2003). *A new look at Black families* (5th ed.). Walnut Creek, CA: Altamira Press.

Wolcott, H. F. (2001). *Writing up qualitative research* (2nd ed.). Thousand Oaks, CA: Sage.

Wright, R. (1945). *Black boy*. New York, NY: Harper & Brothers.

SUBJECT INDEX